MW01290461

Selfhelp for Teens

Confidence, Assertiveness and Self-Esteem Training
(3 in 1)

Simple and Proven Techniques to
Become Your Confident Self
(for Boys and Girls)

By

Maria Van Noord

© Copyright 2018 - All rights reserved.

The content contained within this book may not be reproduced, duplicated or transmitted without direct written permission from the author or the publisher.

Under no circumstances will any blame or legal responsibility be held against the publisher, or author, for any damages, reparation, or monetary loss due to the information contained within this book. Either directly or indirectly.

Legal Notice:

This book is copyright protected. This book is only for personal use. You cannot amend, distribute, sell, use, quote or paraphrase any part, or the content within this book, without the consent of the author or publisher.

Disclaimer Notice:

Please note the information contained within this document is for educational and entertainment purposes only. All effort has been executed to present accurate, up to date, and reliable, complete information. No warranties of any kind are declared or implied. Readers acknowledge that the author is not engaging in the rendering of legal, financial, medical or professional advice. The content within this book has been derived from various sources. Please consult a licensed professional before attempting any techniques outlined in this book.

By reading this document, the reader agrees that under no circumstances is the author responsible for any losses, direct or indirect, which are incurred as a result of the use of information contained within this document, including, but not limited to, — errors, omissions, or inaccuracies.

Table Of Contents

Part 1 Confidence for Teens

Stop Doubting and Stop Stress by Becoming Confident

Using These 3 Simple and Effective Techniques

By

Maria Van Noord

Chapter 1: Introduction: What is Confidence and Why is it Important?

Confidence is a term that refers to a person's awareness of his or her own capabilities. If you are a confident individual, then it means you are aware of your capabilities and feel secure in that knowledge. The security of being confident does not include arrogance. Confidence is related to a realistic acceptance of one's abilities, strengths, and weaknesses.

Confident individuals:
- Have a deep sense of security
- Have a sincere belief in their strengths and skills to overcome challenges as they arise
- Have a sense of preparedness for tests, classes, and competitions
- Believe they can rather than they can't

Confidence can also be understood by comparing it with arrogance and low self-esteem. Confidence is identifying and appreciating what you are good at, the value your skills provide, and behaving in a way that reveals this aspect of your personality to other people. In contrast, arrogance is believing that you are more valuable than you really are; while low self-esteem is believing that you are less worthy than you genuinely are.

There are two ways of looking at confidence: to be confident and to have confidence. Being confident is reflected in your outward appearance. So, when you appear confident in front of other people, you are being confident. This does not necessarily mean you 'have' confidence which is what is inside of you. You need not have confidence and yet be confident in front of others.

This conflicting situation will not last very long because sooner than later, your inner lack of confidence is bound to show up externally as well. Typically, when you have confidence (which is a deep belief in your own capabilities and self-worth), then being confident happens naturally because what is inside is quite easily seen on the outside.

Importance and Benefits of Being Confident

Being confident comes with a host of benefits. It is a beneficial and powerful thing to possess. However, please remember that there is nothing 'right' or 'wrong' about being confident or not being confident. What this means, if you are a person who lacks confidence or are low on confidence then there is nothing to feel bad about.

Accept yourself the way you are, and then work towards improving yourself for your own. Mark Twain said, *'The worst kind of loneliness is when you cannot be comfortable with yourself.'* Instead of feeling bad for the person you are, look at the following excellent benefits of building your confidence level and work at it.

You will have a healthy sense of self-worth – With confidence comes a healthy sense of self-worth. You will find value in yourself and your capabilities which will help you lead your life with your head held high. For example, if you worked hard for a test and cleared it with flying colors, you will be proud of your hard work and achievement which will take your confidence level a few notches up.

Improved happiness and joy – If your sense of self-worth is up and you achieve an increased number of successes, then automatically you will feel happier and more joyful than before. For example, if you have been doing badly in your tests, you would feel low and down in the dumps. Receiving good grades in a test will win you accolades from your peers, teachers, and loved ones which will make you happy.

You will not have self-doubt – The mental torture of self-doubt can be a debilitating factor in your life. Self-doubt creates anxieties and stresses for you as you feel inadequate about your abilities to manage and overcome challenges. In fact, self-doubt is one of the primary reasons for not wanting to try new things. Confidence eliminates self-doubt as you begin to feel valuable.

Improved strength and capabilities – Increased

confidence gives you increased strength and power which, in turn, will provide you with more confidence to face bigger challenges than before. Each new challenge only serves to enhance your strength and capabilities. Even if you failed in any challenge, the learning from those experiences makes your strong; it does not weaken you in any way.

Taking the example of the class test, good grades in one test will drive you to work harder for the next. Hard work invariably leads to improved grades in the next test, and the next, and the next. Each time you do better, your confidence in your learning capabilities will improve.

Confidence attracts people to you – Consider this scenario: you are a new student in school, and you walk into the class on the first day. There are two students already seated. One is looking down with no smile on his face. He looks up furtively at you and looks away immediately. You can make out his lack of confidence. The other boy looks up confidently, makes eye contact, and gives you a warm smile. He exudes confidence. Who will you walk towards? Typically, the second boy, right? That is how confidence attracts people.

Kiesza, the young Canadian multi-instrumentalist and singer, says, *"Beauty comes in a million forms. But the most beautiful thing is confidence."*

Confidence: Genetic Vs. Learned Skill

So, a pertinent question about confidence is: "Are people born confident or can this trait be learned and mastered?" To answer this, ask yourself this question: When you first learned to write full sentences in English, how confident were you with making error-free ones? Now, as a teenager, how confident are you with writing error-free sentences in English? Is this confidence result of your genetic makeup or because of constant writing practice?

Yes, there are genetic factors that, perhaps, make certain people have a higher predisposition to confidence and optimism than others. However, there is little effect of biological factors in the long journey of building this essential skill.

Moreover, your biological factors need not determine your destiny. The option to take control of your destiny is in your hands. Some people have started off gawky teenagers who are low on confidence and ended up blooming into powerful, strong, and confident people based on their healthy habits that built their confidence level. Here are some famous examples:

Helen Keller – It is easy to imagine the enormous challenges this blind and deaf girl would have to overcome as a teenager. She didn't allow her inner fears to control her life. Instead, she turned around and controlled her fears. She grew up to become a famous speaker championing for civil rights, world peace, and birth control.

Thomas Edison – His confidence took a big hit when his teacher told him he was intellectually disabled and should not come to school. Additionally, Edison's physical health was very fragile. And to make matters worse, he became hard of hearing from the age of 12. He never stopped being confident and rose above all these challenges to become one of the greatest inventors of all times.

Gianluigi Donnarumma – This teenage football sensation was signed on by the prestigious AC Milan football club when he was just 14, and made his debut when he was just short of 17. In December 2017, he broke down in public when some fans put up rude and cruel banners against him asking for him to quit. But with the help of his captain, coach, family, and friends, he regained his confidence and is considered to have a very bright future in football.

Confidence and Self-Esteem

Although self-esteem and confidence are used interchangeably, they are different elements. However, the two elements are connected in some ways too. Self-esteem is a term that reflects the value you give yourself in this world. 'Am I a worthwhile individual?' If the answer to this question is 'Yes,' then your self-esteem is fairly high.

Moreover, self-esteem is an element that does not change much over short periods of time. It remains at similar levels in all areas of your life. So, if you have a high self-esteem at work, it is very likely that your self-esteem is the same at home, in your social circle, and other aspects of your life. Self-esteem is a reflection of how you see and value yourself.

Contrarily, confidence is associated with action. You could feel confident doing a particular job but not very confident doing something. You could be a confident father and husband but not a very confident worker at your office. Psychologists term confidence as being domain-specific. For example, you could be confident in doing math but not very confident in writing English essays.

It is easier to build confidence than building self-esteem. You could have great self-esteem but not be confident in life, and vice versa. Take the example of Andre Agassi, the famous tennis player and winner of multiple Grand Slams. He was very confident about his ability to play great games. But, from a self-esteem perspective, he was a man riddled with anxiety, stress, and a low opinion about himself. Therefore, although it is natural that a confident person will also have high self-esteem, that is not always the case.

Confidence and Assertiveness

Assertiveness and confidence are traits that complement each other, and yet are different in many ways. The primary difference between the two traits lies in the aspect of communication. Being assertive requires something or someone to show your assertiveness to. For example, you have to talk to someone or interact with someone to show your assertiveness because it is a perception-based personality trait. However, confidence is more connected with your internal self. You can have confidence without any interaction with anyone outside of yourself.

But, assertiveness cannot truly exist without the underlying confidence. A genuine portrayal of assertiveness through verbal and nonverbal communication can happen only when a person's confidence level is high.

Chapter Summary

Confidence is the awareness of one's own capabilities minus the arrogance. Confidence is a trait that can be learned and mastered through practice. There are multiple benefits of being confident including a more meaningful, happy, and joyful life free from anxieties and self-doubt. Confidence is easier to build than self-esteem. You don't need any external situation or people to have confidence whereas assertiveness needs an external platform to be showcased.

Chapter 2: Understanding Your Current Level of Confidence

Do you know what your current level of confidence is? This information is a key element to move forward or make positive changes. So, this chapter is dedicated to helping you determine your current level of confidence. Then you will be able to properly address what changes you can make in your life to improve your confidence.

Q1. When a math problem is given to me, I am confident I can use the theories learned in class to solve.
1. Never   2. Sometimes   3. Very often   4. Always

Q2. Based on what I have learned in my science class, I am confident I can create experiments.
1. Never   2. Sometimes   3. Very often   4. Always

Q3. During lab activities, I confidently use my theoretical skills to perform experiments successfully.
1. Never   2. Sometimes   3. Very often   4. Always

Q4. I can confidently lead a team to create a class project.
1. Never   2. Sometimes   3. Very often   4. Always

Q5. Even when I don't know the answer immediately, I know where the required information is.
1. Never   2. Sometimes   3. Very often   4. Always

Q6. I can confidently help my friends understand class lessons if they ask me to.
1. Never   2. Sometimes   3. Very often   4. Always

Q7. I am confident of getting good grades in my tests and assignments.
1. Never   2. Sometimes   3. Very often   4. Always

Q8. Would you think of appearing in a quiz show on television?
1. Yes   2. I don't know   3. No

Q9. Would you give a big speech about your favorite historical character in front of your entire grade?
1. Yes   2. I don't know   3. No

Q10. Do you believe you are a positive person?
1. Yes   2. I don't know   3. No

Q11. Would you wish to be the pilot on a plane?
1. Yes   2. I don't know   3. No

Q12. Have you ever disagreed confidently with your parents?

1. Yes   2. I don't know   3. No

Q13. Would you contradict your teacher if you believed you are right?

1. Yes   2. I don't know   3. No

Q14. Do you think attacking first is the best way to save yourself in a war-like situation?

1. Yes   2. I don't know   3. No

Q15. Are you confident of crossing the road?

1. Yes   2. I don't know   3. No

Q16. Would you take a boat ride into the beach even if it looked like there is going to be a storm?

1. Yes   2. I don't know   3. No

Q17. If you had to choose between two tasks one being more difficult than the other, would you choose the more difficult one?

1. Yes   2. I don't know   3. No

Q18. Do you think you are cleverer than the average student in your class?

1. Yes   2. I don't know   3. No

Q19. Would you dismantle a mechanical toy feeling confident that you can put it back together again?

1. Yes   2. I don't know   3. No

Q20. Are you impressed with good speakers in your school and wish you could speak as well as they do?

1. Yes   2. I don't know   3. No

Q21. If you are alone at home at night because your parents have gone off to a party, and you hear a sound in the kitchen, would you go and investigate?

1. Yes   2. I don't know   3. No

Q22. Do you do things to please others even if you don't like to do these things?

1. Never   2. Sometimes   3. Very often   4. Always

Q23. If a good friend criticizes you badly in front of others, would you speak out against the friend?

1. Never   2. Sometimes   3. Very often   4. Always

Q24. Suppose you are at a party in which a boy/girl you have a crush on also comes. Would you go up and talk to the person?

1. Never   2. Sometimes   3. Very often   4. Always

Q25. How often are you positive about your capabilities?

1. Never   2. Sometimes   3. Very often   4. Always

Q26. When you are talking to your classmates, do you make eye contact with them?

1. Never   2. Sometimes   3. Very often   4. Always

Q27. When you are talking to people whom you are not particularly fond of, do you make eye contact with them?
1. Never   2. Sometimes   3. Very often   4. Always

Q28. Suppose you went to another school for a debate as an audience, and someone misbehaved with one of your schoolmates. Would you take an effort to register a complaint?
1. Never   2. Sometimes   3. Very often   4. Always

Q29. Are you happy with the skills you have picked up in school until now?
1. Yes   2. I don't know   3. No

Q30. Do you depend on other people to feel happy about yourself?
1. Yes   2. I don't know   3. No

Q31. Do you try new things easily and without much persuasion?
1. Yes   2. I don't know   3. No

Q32. Do you take yourself out of your comfort zone often?
1. Yes   2. I don't know   3. No

Self-Discovery with a Partner

Another effective way to understand your current level of confidence is to take the help of a trusted friend or family member. If it is a friend, a joint self-discovery project might be worthwhile. Think of a situation (real or imaginary) which requires confidence to be displayed; for example, suppose it was an impromptu speech to be given in front of strangers.

Now, each of you write down how you believe you will behave in such a situation. Make notes of the following elements:

- Your emotions; will you be scared or confident?

_____

_____

_____

_____

_____

_____

Friend's comments

_____

_____

_____

_____

- How will you go about managing your emotions?

_____

_____

_____

_____

Friend's comments

_____

_____

_____

_____

_____

- Your level of preparedness; will the impromptu situation drive you into a panic or not?

_____

_____

_____

_____

_____

Friend's comments

_____

_____

_____

_____

_____

- Will you think that you will be able to handle the situation if the audience consisted of known people?

_____

_____

_____

_____

_____

Friend's comments

_____

_____

_____

_____

_____

Now, exchange the written notes with your friend. Read what your friend has written and write your own comments next to your friend's thoughts. Add something he or she might have missed out. Remove something if you believe that is not what your friend would have done. Similarly, your friend should do the same with your notes.

This exercise will give you an idea of whether your perception of yourself matches with what others have of you. This knowledge will help you understand if your confidence level is aligned with your skill levels. For example, if you had written that you would be scared about such a situation, and your friend disagreed and believed that you would actually sail through the impromptu speech, then it means you are not connected correctly with your inner skills. Regarding such conflicting situations ask yourself these questions:

- Do I present my skills genuinely to outsiders? Am I more skilled than I believe myself to be? Or is it vice versa?
- Do I see myself differently from how others see me?

If your own ideas and that of your friend's match, then it is simple to know where your current level of confidence stands.

Chapter Summary

Answer each of the questions honestly and to the best of your abilities. Using the information from these self-discovery exercises you will be able to gauge your current level of confidence and the areas you need to improve.

Chapter 3: Growth Mindset for Confidence

So, how does one begin to become confident? The first thing to do to start your confidence-building journey is to decide to change. The decision to do something is always the first step in the path to achieving the goal. It is the same with confidence-building. Start today at this moment with the thought. 'I am confident, and I will work every day to become increasingly confidently.'

There are two critical things to build confidence over a period of time. They include:

- Start by building a growth mindset
- Learn and practice skills in which you lack confidence until you become a master

Growth Mindset

You start your confidence-building journey with the decision that you are confident from now on, and you will work hard every day to continue to be confident. However, the path can be fraught with obstacles and challenges. Confidence is a state of mind that keeps fluctuating depending on your moods, circumstances, physical health, and a host of other reasons. It is essential to develop a growth mindset to keep your confidence level high irrespective of the external circumstances.

Growth mindset Vs. fixed mindset – Carol S. Dweck, a Stanford University professor and researcher coined these two terms and described them in detail. Here are some pointers to understand the difference between the two:

A fixed mindset person is one who believes his or her intelligence, capabilities, and talents are fixed and cannot undergo change. So, if you are a fixed mindset teenager, you probably think that you are good only at certain things and not at all useful at other things, and no matter what you do, you are not going to change.

Students with a fixed mindset believe that if they look unintelligent even once in front of people, then they cannot redeem themselves of this profile, and will always appear dumb. Such people are under a lot of stress because of their rigid belief system that prevents growth.

Contrarily, a person with a growth mindset believes that abilities, intelligence, and talents can be developed through hard work, effort, and persistence. If you are a growth mindset student, then you believe that even if you are not doing well in math today, with a bit of effort, hard work, and persistent, you can become a math whizz soon enough. As a growth mindset teenager, you believe in the idea (which is true, by the way) that anyone can get do things better than they are currently doing if they persist and try hard enough.

Rico Love, the famous American singer, songwriter, producer, and a highly influential figure in the music world says, *"The right mindset is needed for success. I know a lot of people who are more talented than I am. But, driven by their fixed mindset, they do not work hard."*

So, if you are a fixed mindset teenager, and you lack confidence, then you are under a misconception that you can never have confidence. Thus, the first step to building confidence is to change your mindset from fixed to growth. Here are some tips to help you develop a growth mindset.

Acknowledge and accept your weaknesses – For example, you know that you may be lazy. There have been many occasions in which this laziness trait has caused you difficulties and pains. Don't try to find an excuse for this problem. Acknowledge and accept its presence.

Treat obstacles as opportunities – The bigger the challenges, the greater is our potential for growth. So, if you are stuck with fears before choosing a difficult class or trying out something you've never done before, tell yourself that this obstacle is an opportunity for growth and development.

Staying in your comfort zone will not only prevent your learning, growth, and development but also could make you resentful about missing opportunities in the future.

Identify your learning style – Each person has different learning styles. Some students absorb information efficiently when they hear it being said. Some others prefer to have visual aids for better learning. And there are some who can learn only when they read from a book and make notes.

Find what you suits you best, and ensure all study strategies are centered on this unique learning style. This knowledge will enhance the joy of learning and make your school days very meaningful.

First learn, then worry about seeking approval from others – You should not study because you want to get good grades. You must focus on studying because you want to learn and know more about this universe and how it works. This style of learning will not put you under undue pressure about how good your grades are which is what others use to give you approval.

Focus on improving your knowledge and grades will take care of themselves. A desire to learn is a critical step to developing a growth mindset which, in turn, brings success in your life. The legendary footballer, Pele, said, '*Success is not an accident. It is the result you get when you combine hard work, study, commitment, practice, sacrifice, and persistent efforts.*'

In this same space, it makes sense also to tell you that seek to learn well instead of learning fast. Learning well will ensure you don't forget lessons for a long time, and you can leverage the power of that knowledge for an extended period of time. Moreover, when you choose to learn well and deeply instead of fast and frivolously, you will focus on the process of the learning and not on the end result which is another important trait for a growth mindset.

Don't be afraid of making mistakes – Never let the fear of making mistakes prevent you from learning and growing. In fact, the best way to handle the challenges of potential errors is to be mentally prepared that things are bound to go wrong somewhere, sometime. Making mistakes is a natural process of human life. Yes, making mistakes might hurt in some way but also beneficial in many ways including:

- It keeps us grounded. It frees us from the delusion of perfectionism. Although we know we are not the best, when we make mistakes we find easier to absorb this truth. The learning that comes from making mistakes is not to be undermined in any way. Therefore, always remember that undertaking any venture will always result in either a win or a lesson; never a loss.

- Mistakes help us be more compassionate to ourselves than before. Research studies prove that being kind to ourselves helps us move forward and improve our learning and development.

- Failing a test could actually remove the fear of failure. Once you have experienced failure, then the fear of failure ceases to worry you. In the absence of fear, you feel relieved and are willing to take more risks than before thereby opening up your growth opportunities.

- Hitting a snag in our journey can help in motivating us to work harder and do better. It might sound counterproductive. But, in truth, if our journey is very smooth with no hitches, we hit a boredom curve which potentially results in reduced motivation in the task at hand. Failures wake us up from this feeling of boredom and recharge us.

25

Use these tips to build a growth mindset and jump into the important journey of confidence-building.

Learn and Practice New Skills

Learn and practice skills in which you lack confidence until you become a master. This is the second most effective way to build confidence. Here are some tips to help build your skills in such a way that your expertise contributes to your confidence.

Always have a curious attitude – For example, if your teacher has taught you the basics of a particular math topic, don't stop there. Go home and see if you can read up more about that topic. Curiosity enhances the joy of learning and developing skills and your mind will absorb the knowledge at a deeper level than otherwise: Some tips to build curiosity:

- Avoid saying something is boring or dull; use of this word kills curiosity like nothing else
- Develop a questioning attitude; keep asking why, how, what, why not, when, etc.
- Always dig deeper than below the surface

Increase your versatility quotient – Being good at multiple skills improves your confidence significantly as your abilities are appreciated by more people than if you were skilled at only one thing. Tips to build versatility:

- Learn to adapt quickly to new and even seemingly

uncomfortable situations

- Learn to work smart and not hard
- Spend time with other skilled people and learn how they do things
- Spend a lot of time reading books on a variety of topics

Identify role models – It is always easy to grow and develop if you have someone a role model to replicate. Role models give you a foundation on which you build your own skills and abilities. They are a standard based on which you can track your progress.

Lana Del Ray, the American songwriter, singer, and producer who started her musical career with the viral success of her single, 'Video Games' at the age of 21, says, *'Find a person whose life you want; then, figure out how they got it, and replicate their efforts. Choose your role models wisely and do what they did.'*

Identify mentors – Role models could be people whom you cannot really interact with on a daily basis. Ideally, your role should be your mentor too. However, it is not always possible. For example, if you are a computer geek and want to become like Bill Gates, then he is your role model.

But, you need a mentor who will help you overcome daily challenges in your journey to becoming like your role model. Typically, as a teenager, your parents, a favorite teacher, a senior in school, an older sibling or any well-wisher whom you trust implicitly can be your mentor.

Chapter Summary

In this chapter, you learned the importance and benefits of developing a growth mindset and building and expanding your skill sets to increase your confidence levels. Most importantly, the journey to building confidence starts with your decision to be confident today, and every day henceforth.

Chapter 4: Self-Awareness - Know Your Core Values

Let us start this chapter by understanding what core values are. There are a lot of things you value in your life including your parents, friends, perhaps a couple of teachers, coaches, and more. These people are of value to you because they make your life truly worthwhile.

Core values, sometimes referred to as personal values, are those personality traits or qualities that not just worthy of living a good and morally uplifting life but also are the driving force for your goals and life purpose. Core values:

- Help you set up priorities in your life
- Are key influencers to making critical every day decisions
- Are connected to your personal conviction that is close to your heart or something that you feel very strongly about
- Help you make life choices
- Are sometimes legacies carried forward from your parents and grandparents and those that you wish to hand over to the next generation in the family
- Help you manage your resources, especially time and

energy, wisely and prudently; you can focus your resources only on those elements that are aligned with your core values and not waste them on other elements.

- Helps you build your level of assertiveness as you battle with yourself and the world around you to live by core values

Core values provide you with a sense of focus in your life. They help set up boundaries in life so that you can stay on your path without being unduly distracted. For example, if you take discipline as one of your core values, then following your study schedule each day will become an activity that is guided by this particular core value.

Suppose your friends pester you to come for parties regularly and you choose to agree to go each time, then your daily study schedule will be negatively impacted which is in direct conflict with your core value of leading a disciplined life. Therefore, this particular core value will help you keep your boundaries for such distractions, and stand firm on your principles and say no to distracting parties.

Characteristics of Core Values

As a teenager, it is quite likely that you are yet to define core values for yourself. The fact that you have the mindset to access and read books such as this one reflects a maturity level that belies your age.

Being able to set your core values so early on in life will help you a meaningful purpose for yourself; something that will last an entire lifetime. Before going on to give you ideas on how to choose your core values, here are some of their standard characteristics:

Typically, your ability to implement your core values should not depend on your physical condition – That means to say, a core value such as leading a disciplined life can be done irrespective of your physical state; you could be rich or poor, you could be physically strong or weak; irrespective of your physical state you can live a disciplined life.

However, physical fitness cannot be a core value because you cannot really implement it if you are sick or stuck in a place that does not give you the necessary requirements to be physically fit.

Core values should not depend on any external factors – For example, a core value like getting the highest grade in the class at all times cannot be a core value because you have to depend on others to get lesser grades than you. You can study hard and get great grades. However, you have no control over someone else to get better grades than you.

Similarly, wanting to be popular cannot be a core value because you need other people to make you popular. However, courage can be a core value because you don't need anybody else to be brave and courageous.

Self-Assessment Exercise to Find Your Core Values

Identify the list of core values that are important to you. You can choose from over 400 core values including love, discipline, honesty, integrity, prudence, ambition, health, fun, respect, friendship, family, balance, and more. However, instead of choosing core values randomly from this rather large list, it is best to look at your past experiences and pick up critical ideas that have helped drive your life until now. Here are some tips for that:

Write down the top five best experiences in your life – Give a name to each of these experiences and answer the following questions for every one of the chosen five:

Describe the experience including the time, your age, and what exactly happened.

_____

_____

_____

_____

_____

What were the topmost emotions that you were feeling at that time?

_____

_____

_____

_____

_____

Write down the thoughts that were going on in your head from memory

_____

_____

_____

_____

_____

What were the values of life that were in play during that time? Many times, you may not have known the core value by name. Now, however, when you are thinking about that experience specifically, the core values that were part of that experience will leap out at you.

_____

_____

_____

_____

_____

Write down the worst five experiences in your life – For each of these events in your life, answer them as for the best experiences of your life except the last one. The last question will be reworded as, "What were the values of life that were suppressed during that time?" So, here is the worksheet to complete answering the questions regarding the worst five experiences:

Describe the experience including the time, your age, and what   exactly   happened

_____

_____

_____

_____

_____

What were the topmost emotions that you were feeling at that time?

_____

_____

_____

_____

_____

Write down the thoughts that were going on in your head from memory

_____

_____

_____

_____

_____

What were the values of life that were suppressed during that time?

_____

_____

_____

_____

_____

Write down your code of conduct – To get answers for this, you must ask yourself the question, "After the basic human needs including food, clothing, shelter, good home, good school, etc. (all of which are likely being provided by your parents or guardian at this point in your life), what are the next set of essential elements essential to lead my life meaningfully?" Here are some examples to get you going:

- Vitality and health
- Nature and its beauty
- Creativity
- Adventure and excitement

- Learning

Gather together similar core values - From the list of values garnered from the above three steps, combine similar core values together. Here some examples to help you understand better:

- Accomplishment, achievement, ambition, productivity, and other things can be combined under 'result-oriented'
- Altruism, generosity, goodness, helpful, and other related values can be combined under 'service-oriented'

From this combined lot, choose the top few only. It is best to keep your core value list between 5 and 10. A number bigger than 10 will make it difficult for you to keep track of and a number smaller than 5 will not cover all the important aspects of life values.

Once you have the list of core values in place, rank them in order of importance in your life. This step might take a little longer than you thought. It is quite natural to be confused with putting core values in order of importance since all of them will look equally important to you. It might be a good idea to revisit your best and worst experiences for this exercise. You could get some insight into subtler layers of your emotions that will help you in the ranking exercise.

For example, suppose one of your best experiences was getting great grades in your final class examination, and you have attributed core values of disciplined study for that. Suppose your second-best experience was fighting off a bully successfully, and for this your core value was courage. Now, to rank courage and discipline, revisit your experiences and try to analyze which experience was the better one, and you could use that feeling to rank these two core values.

It is a trial and error method and could take a few days to completely and satisfactorily get your core values listed and ranked in order of priority. Keep this core value list in clearly visible places. Every time you are in a dilemma about any decision-making, look at this list. Making the decision will be faster and easier than before.

Chapter Summary

Here you learned the importance and benefits of having a set of core values. You learned that decision-making, especially during dilemmas, is eased considerably if you have core values to guide you. Core values help you stay on the path of success and your chosen goals. You also learned the key characteristics of core values and how to choose them and rank them in order of priority in your own life.

Chapter 5: Setting Goals to Achieve Your Mission and Purpose

Now that you have got your core values clearly embedded in your psyche, it is time to set goals for your life. You have to have a mission and purpose to lead a meaningful and fulfilling life. Before we go into how to set goals in your life, let look at the importance of goal-setting.

Importance of Mission or Purpose and Goals In Your Life

Purpose or mission and goal are words that are commonly used interchangeably. However, there are some basic differences. One of the primary difference is that goals are invariably connected to time. For example, your goal for this year in school might be to get a GPA score of 3.5 or more.

Purpose, on the other hand, is the reason to achieve this particular goal. In this case, your purpose as a teenager would be to have a good adult life in the future free from financial burden. Your purpose is achieved by meeting timed goals. Despite these subtle differences, purpose and goals are deeply connected with each other.

A goal can be defined as the desired outcome you envision, plan, and commit to. Some goals have a finite time limit through various deadlines. Typically, any planning you do regarding your future can be called a goal of your life. Even something as simple as planning to catch that new movie over the weekend with your friends or going to the Saturday-night party is a goal for you.

Therefore, every day, week, month, and year should ideally have goals set and plans in place on how to achieve the set goals. There are many useful reasons for goal-setting including:

Goals render focus to your efforts – Can you shoot an arrow without a target? The same holds good for life too. You cannot thoughtlessly put in efforts without knowing what you want at the end of it. You should have an aim or goal to prevent your efforts from becoming wasteful or useless.

A classic example is the effort of the sunlight. It will warm everything it comes in contact with. But, use a magnifying glass to focus sunlight's energy, and it will be able to create a fire. So, like the magnifying glass, goals form the direction of your life.

Goals help you track your progress – When you envision a goal, you have an endpoint in sight. As you work towards achieving the goal, you can easily measure if you have made progress by calculating the remaining distance between you and your goal.

For example, suppose on Monday morning, you have set yourself a goal of studying three chapters in Math by the end of Friday of the same week. You have chosen to break up your weekly goal into daily goals to track progress. At the end of each day, you will know how close you are to achieving your weekly goal of three chapters.

Goals rescue you from distractions – Goals act like boundaries preventing you from falling for distractions. When your mind is tuned for a predetermined end result, it automatically senses distractions and keeps away from them.

For example, suppose you have a first date with someone at 8 PM. You are to meet with your date at a restaurant which is a 15-minute walk from your home. You finished your chores at home including, perhaps, class assignments due for tomorrow, and you leave at around 7:45 for your meeting.

It is only natural that you will focus on your walking, and in fact, ensure you keep it at a brisk pace to reach a couple of minutes before 8 because you don't want to be late for your first date, right? That is the power of setting a goal. You don't stray from your path.

Goals prevent procrastination – Self-committed goals are great tools to prevent procrastination. Compare a self-committed goal against a passing whim. Goals stick in your head and keep rattling the cage if you try to procrastinate whereas passing whims tend to be forgotten as it doesn't matter if you achieve it or not.

Self-Discovery Questions before You Set Goals

Before you set goals, ask yourself the following questions and write down the answers so that you can refer to them as you move forward in your goal-setting journey. In fact, the answers to these questions could serve to be your mission and purpose of your teenage which can then be used to complete the daily, weekly, and monthly goal-setting worksheets given below.

How do I define a meaningful life? This may seem like a difficult question to answer straight away. Use these questions to help you find answers. What moves and drives me to work hard? What are the things that I care about? What are my desires?

_____

_____

_____

_____

_____

_____

What are my past experiences that are worth remembering, both good and bad? The answers to this question will give you an insight into the primary question of: Where have I been before?

_____

_____

_____

_____

_____

Where am I right now? For this question, reflect on the answers to What kind of a person am I? What are my abilities? What are my strengths and weaknesses? What do I love doing? What do I hate doing?

_____

_____

_____

_____

_____

_____

_____

Where do I want to be in the next 5-6 years? For this, think about questions such as What are the abilities or skills I want to learn and master? What are the learning goals I have to set for myself?

_____

_____

_____

_____

_____

_____

_____

What are the steps I need to get there? What are the resources I need to get for myself? What are the impending obstacles? How can I overcome them? Who can help me in achieving my goals? What are the elements that are holding me back?

_____

_____

_____

_____

_____

_____

_____

How will I measure my progress? How will I know I have reached where I wanted to?

_____

_____

_____

_____

_____

_____

Daily Goals Worksheet for Teenagers

Before sleeping each night, complete the following daily goal-setting sheet:

My primary goal for tomorrow is:

_____

_____

_____

_____

The steps I am taking to achieve this goal are:

_____

_____

_____

_____

Here are some classic examples for teenagers that you should include into your daily goal list:

- Make my bed – Yes, it brings a sense of order right from when you wake up
- Go for a run or walk
- Read one chapter and answer a few questions in English, Science, Social Science, or any other subject
- Do a set number of math problems
- Practice music or a sport for at least 30 minutes
- Complete homework before 8 PM

Weekly Goals Worksheet for Teenagers

This should ideally be done at the end of Sunday.
My goals for this week are:

_____

_____

_____

_____

_____

_____

Steps that should be taken to achieve my weekly goals are:

_____

_____

_____

_____

_____
_____
_____

Typically, your weekly goals should be divided into daily goals. For example, completing three chapters for an upcoming test in English, Science, Social Science, any other subject could be a weekly goal which you have divided into daily goals in the daily goal worksheet.

Monthly Goals Worksheet for Teenagers

My goals for this month are:

_____
_____
_____
_____
_____
_____
_____

Steps I will take to achieve my monthly goals are:

_____
_____
_____
_____
_____
_____

Typically, your monthly goals should be divided into

weekly and then daily goals. For example, completing the portions for the semester exam for a particular subject could be the monthly goal which you have divided into weekly and daily goals.

Chapter Summary

In this self-awareness chapter, you learned about the cruciality of having a purpose and goal-setting in your life. Complete the questionnaires and use the examples to set your life goals aligned with your core values. Divide your goals into small daily, weekly, and monthly actionable items that you can keep track of and measure.

Chapter 6: Tips and Tricks to Build Confidence - Part I

The next three chapters are dedicated to giving you some tips and tricks to help build your confidence levels.

Building Confidence through Affirmations

Affirmations are positive statements that we tell ourselves repeatedly to bring about positive changes in our lives. Affirmations help in altering our belief systems by getting rid of limiting beliefs and imbibing positive and progressive beliefs. In fact, affirmations are natural psychological tools inbuilt in our system.

For example, when your teacher pulls you up for an error, have you noticed telling yourself, "All will be fine. I should not worry." That is a classic example of affirmations that helps you respond positively even to criticism.

Benefits of daily affirmations – Affirmations are more than merely self-help statements. They can impact the quality of our thoughts significantly resulting in

47

positivity within and outside of you. Repeating affirmations regularly empower you to be in tune with your thoughts which, in turn, helps you to understand yourself better.

The more in tune you are with yourself, the more acutely aware you become to elements that make you happy and those that come in the way of your happiness. This self-awareness gives you the power to make wise decisions in your life that result in happiness.

Moreover, affirmations keep you in a positive and optimistic mood at all times. Positive-thinking and optimistic people tend to be happier, more efficient, and more productive than negative-thinking and pessimistic people. So, here are some amazing confidence-building affirmations you can use on a daily basis.

- I inhale confidence and exhale cowardliness
- I love to meet strangers enthusiastically and boldly
- I love myself deeply and completely; I approve of myself and don't need anyone else's approval to be happy
- I live in the moment and know for sure that the future is good for me
- I exude confidence; I am outgoing and bold
- I am persistent, creative, and innovative in all my endeavors
- I am enthusiastic and energetic; confidence comes naturally to me.
- I am the most positive person in my life and I attract only the best things and people into my life
- I am a problem-solver. When I hear of problems, my

focus is always on the solutions

- I love problems and challenges and treat them as opportunities for learning and growth.
- I am well-groomed and confident-looking. My outer profile matches my inner confidence
- I thrive on confidence. The more confident I am, the easier it is to solve problems
- I counter challenges bravely and confidently. I always find a way out of difficulty and tricky situations
- I use my teacher's criticisms effectively to improve myself
- Today and every day, my desire to learn and grow continues to expand.

Start each morning and end each day by repeating a couple of your favorite affirmations and watch your confidence grow slowly but surely.

Building Confidence through Visualizations

Visualizations and mental imageries are powerful tools that help improve the mental health of teenagers. Jim Carrey, one of the most successful Hollywood actors of the modern times, used visualization techniques to help build his confidence level at the beginning of his career when offers did not come pouring in, and especially on days when things went more wrong than right.

He said, *"I would sit in his car every night and visualize a scene when directors clamored to work with him. I visualized people respecting me for my talent. I visualized positive things happening to me. In those days, I had nothing. But these mental images filled me with confidence and drove me to work harder than before."*

How do we benefit from visualizing what we desire? Research studies have proven that when we imagine something in our head, the primal parts of the brain behave like as if the imagination scene was really happening. Positive visualizations, therefore, impact the entire nervous system. So, if you picture yourself sitting calmly on a beach watching the beautiful serene scene of the setting sun, you automatically feel relaxed.

Using this power, it makes sense to employ the power of visualization to increase your level of confidence. Here are some examples for you:

Visualization example #1 - Suppose you are nervous about asking a girl to go out for a date with you. You have already planned out a conversation strategy to approach her. But the lack of confidence is preventing you from taking a positive step.

Now, here is your visualization scenario:

- Sit comfortably in a quiet place where you will not be disturbed for a while.
- Close your eyes to prevent being distracted by other things around you.
- Imagine the scene where you are walking confidently to the girl. You are neatly turned out. You look good, and you have a nice, warm smile on your face
- Imagine yourself greeting her with a cheery hello.
- Imagine the smile on her face.
- Visualize asking her out on a date even as you mouth

50

the words you have prepared

- Visualize her thinking for a moment, and then agreeing

Keep visualizing this happy scene. You will notice your nervousness will slowly but surely disappear, and you will build the confidence to make this mental image a reality.

Visualization example #2 – Suppose you are being bullied by a group of boys in your class, and you want to voice your resentment strongly and firmly. Being a bit on the passive side, you are not able to find your voice. Now, use this visualization technique to help build confidence to raise your voice. First, make a short speech of what you want to say. Learn it well. Next, sit in a quiet place, close your eyes, and visualize the following scenes:

- Imagine you are walking on the corridor of your school.
- Visualize these bullies walking toward you from the opposite side
- Visualize yourself being confident and strong
- Now, imagine they come close, and even before they start to bully you, you stand firm and say the prepared speech assertively to them.
- Visualize the shock on their faces as you walk away confidently from there.

Challenge Yourself Continuously

There is an anonymous saying that goes like this, "If something doesn't challenge you, then it doesn't change you too." The famous British actor Benedict Cumberbatch says, "The further you move from yourself, the more challenges you will face; the more challenges you face, the more fun you will have."

Remaining in your comfort zone is one of the easiest ways of falling back on building confidence. Your comfort zone gives you the coziness that prevents you from taking risks, a key element in your growth and development. The more you get out of your comfort zone and take on new challenges, the better your confidence.

Accomplishing new challenges and projects, doing unfamiliar stuff, making decisions, and helping others are all activities that increase confidence. However, please remember that you have to first help yourself before you choose to help others.

Work on your skills, become a master, and then help others. For example, if you are have dating issues, sort out your problems first before choosing to help your friend who is having similar challenges. Here are some tips to help you challenge yourself continuously:

Identify your biggest fears and face them continuously for one week – For example, if you are scared of doing Math, then for one week continuously do at least 5 problems each day from the most challenging chapter. You will notice that your math skill will improve with repeated practice.

Do something you hate for a while – If you hate dancing, join a dancing class. If you hate athletics, race with friends who are athletes. If you hate cooking, take a cooking class or better still help your mom in the kitchen. If you don't like a person in your class, make an effort to approach him or her and have a simple conversation.

Do things differently – For example, if you are right-handed, use your left hand to eat, brush your teeth, and other routine jobs of the day.

Stay away from technology a while – In today's tech world, staying away from your mobile devices would be a huge challenge. You need not start with an entire day. Just keep your mobile away for a couple of hours at first. You will notice how your hands are itching to reach out every 5 minutes for the device. Be aware of this desire, and fight it. With each passing hour, you will see how easy life truly becomes without the mobile.

Chapter Summary

In this chapter, you learned three different ways to build confidence including repeating daily affirmations, visualization techniques, and by challenging yourself and getting out of your comfort zone. Building confidence is not a magic trick. It takes time and effort. Persist in your efforts even if you think you are not seeing success, and sooner than later, success will come. Never give up.

Chapter 7: Tips and Tricks to Build Confidence - Part II

Positive Attitude

Having a positive attitude is one of the key elements to building confidence. Be positive about your accomplishments. Focus on the positive events, things, and people in your life, and there will be more of that in your life. Life gives you what you focus on. Don't worry excessively about what people think of you. There are numerous benefits to having a positive attitude including:

Improved levels of motivation – You will feel an increased
level of motivation when you keep a positive attitude which, in turn, will help you accomplish goals and overcome challenges thereby increasing your confidence levels.

Obstacles become opportunities – You will see obstacles as opportunities when you have a positive attitude. The positivity in your perspective will help you see things that are invisible to people with a negative attitude. Seeing obstacles as opportunities makes you creative too because your vision has broadened helping you understand more elements in the situation than before.

Improved self-esteem – A positive outlook enhances your self-belief and confidence in your abilities thereby raising your self—esteem.

Reduced stress – Negative thoughts fill your mind and body with negativity leading to undue and excessive stress which results in the scattering and wasting of energy. When you think positively, this kind of stress is reduced automatically, and your energies are focused on doing productive work.

Moreover, positive thinking creates a positive vibration in your body and mind which enhances your energy levels considerably as compared to a person with a negative attitude. You will be able to accomplish a lot more things in life with this increased level of energy.

So, how to have a positive attitude? Here are some suggestions:

Be a proactive person – Give some thoughts to the future and see how things are likely to unfold. For example, suppose you've had a big fight with your best friend on Friday before school closed for the weekend. On Monday morning, before leaving for school, spend a little bit of time on how you think your first interaction with him or her is going to unfold.

Think about the fight and what are the things you did

wrong. Be proactive and choose to start the conversation by apologizing for those errors. When your friend hears your apology, the chances that he or she also apologizes for his or her mistakes are very high. Positivity is usually contagious.

Similarly, pre-empt possible future events to be best prepared to handle them instead of waiting for bad things to happen, and reacting negatively to them. Of course, you cannot always be right about what will unfold. For such situations, think about what has happened, take a little bit of time, and respond positively. Avoid reacting impulsively.

Live in the moment – Each moment is beautiful. Don't fret about the uncertain future and don't worry excessively about what has happened in the past. Just live in the moment and savor it wholeheartedly. Be happy for the good things and let go of things that affect you negatively. Don't let negativity drag you down.

Make a journal of the good things in your life – Every time something nice happened to you, diarize it for posterity. Do this as a lifelong activity. Every time you feel sad, angry, or upset, just read the good things of your life, and your mood will perk up.

Have a grateful attitude – Gratitude is one of the most effective ways of being positive. When you see the good things in your life, you automatically feel grateful for them, and look at life with a positive attitude. In fact, a sense of gratitude immediately uplifts your spirits. Tips to show gratitude regularly:

- Be a good and active listener. You are being thankful to people when you truly listen to what they are saying
- Give out compliments. When you meet people, find something nice to say about them; a lovely smile, a great shirt, a job well done, etc.
- Let people know your appreciation. Don't just say thank you. Explain in detail how much you appreciate their presence in your life and how many ways they have helped you in the past.
- Write handwritten notes of gratitude instead of sending an electronic message through your phone or computer. This tip is easily possible for someone who you interact with every day such as your teachers, your friends, your parents, and others.

Surround yourself with positivity – Avoid people who have a negative outlook on life. Being around and inspired by confident people increases confidence. Don't be jealous, but copy and learn from them.

Avoid Perfectionism

Doing things to the best of your abilities is one thing. Trying to achieve perfectionism is quite another. Perfectionism can be a huge deterrent to confidence building. As an obsessive perfectionist, you could be plagued by the following emotions and thoughts (all of which eat into your confidence):

- You are not okay with your present self
- Your feelings of satisfaction are always temporary no matter what you achieve
- You see the world in black and white; you only know

success and failure; there are no such things as good enough or close enough

- You think that if all the external things are perfect, you will feel peaceful and happy
- You have to continuously achieve and do great things to feel happy and satisfied
- If you have not achieved at your predetermined level of success, then you are unhappy with the result
- Intention and efforts are not sufficient. You must get successful and great results. You focus on the product and never on the process

Here are some challenges associated with trying to be a perfectionist:

Troubled relationships – Your relationships may suffer because your expectations can be challengingly unreasonable making your friends, partners, siblings, and other people in your life feel inadequate and stressed out. As a perfectionist, you are always finding fault with your date or friend or anyone else.

Always anxious and tired – Your obsession to overachieve and do everything perfectly will put you on high-alert at all times, driving up your level of anxiety considerably. This always-on-high-alert situation will leave you tired and exhausted most of the time.

Always filled with a sense of guilt and shame – As a perfectionist, you are intolerant to disorganization, mess, clutter, mistakes, and other perfectly human elements. You treat the outside world to be a reflection of your inner self. So, if you see a mess on the outside, you don't feel safe and good. This attitude can drive you to feel a sense of shame and guilt at all times because it is impossible to be utterly and spotlessly perfect always.

Stop being Ms. or Mr. Perfect, if you make mistakes and dare to share them and what you learned from them with other people will have more respect for you. Here are some tips to overcome a perfectionist attitude which does far more harm than good for you:

Learn to be happy with good enough – Being happy with good enough does not mean you slack off. It is only a means to avoid being obsessively perfect. There is a good-enough level in everything we do. Find the right balance between slacking off and being good enough without wasting undue resources on trying to be overly perfect. You will have to use a trial and error method to find the right balance needed to make you happy with good enough.

Accept that perfectionism is a myth – There is nothing called absolute perfectionism. Being perfect is only relative. What is good enough for you is perfect for someone else, and what is bad for you is good enough for someone else. In fact, obsessing over perfection can cause harm both to you and your loved ones.

Remember you cannot ace your tests all the time. And even if you manage to ace them, it does not mean you know the subject like an expert. Do your best and continue to do your best.

Accept that you are human and mistakes are part

of human life – Everyone and everything in this human world has flaws and things are bound to go wrong many times. Look at the mistakes in the right perspective (reread *'don't be scared of mistakes'* subsection in Chapter 3 to understand the importance of mistakes) and learn from them and move on.

And most importantly, life will not reject you if you are imperfect. Reasonably balanced and mature people appreciate the value of mistakes and the dangers of perfectionism and will never reject you for lacking so-called 'perfectionism.'

Always compare yourself only to yourself – At every level of progress, make sure you have done ample work needed to better your previous level. Don't compare yourself with others. Each one's life is unique. You lead yours to the best of your abilities and let others lead theirs to their best of their capabilities.

Chapter Summary

In this chapter, you learned how to build confidence by cultivating a positive attitude and by avoiding perfectionism.

Chapter 8: Tips and Tricks to Build Confidence - Part III

Practice Self-Love and Self-Respect

Respect yourself, so you do not need others to respect you. Love yourself first before you love others. In fact, when you learn self-love and self-respect, you will automatically be able to love and respect others too.

Self-love is not about narcissism or being self-centered or self-absorbed. Self-love is loving and accepting yourself the way you are. It is a trait that gives us the control of our own power while helping us treat others and ourselves compassionately and respectfully. Here are some amazing benefits and side-effects of self-love:

- We are freed from anger, shame, and blame. We can access our inner power to the fullest and invite love into our lives
- It does not matter what others think of us; we learn to believe in our power and strength
- We are at peace as we accept ourselves completely; since we don't have to maintain a façade for the sake of the outside world, we are freed from the associated

stress.

- We become responsible for our happiness and joys. We recognize the universal truth that we are the source and reason for whatever is happening in our lives.
- As we learn to love ourselves better, we get rid of loneliness. We find comfort and joy being by ourselves. This means we don't need to depend on anyone else for our happiness and contentment.
- The more we love and respect ourselves, the more we are able to love and respect others.
- We feel safe and secure because we know we will always be there for ourselves. We are freed from fear

So, how can you practice self-love and self-respect? Here are a few tips to help you:

Create a community for yourself – Although each of us is capable of self-love, it is important to have people who are like-minded and love you for who you are. As a teenager, building a community of such people for such people for yourself will help you right through your life. The friends and community you build during your adolescents invariably last you an entire lifetime.

Make a list of things in your life that make you happy – Look at your life closely and list down the things that really make you happy. When you see an abundance of things that you love in your life and make you happy then you will find multiple reasons to love and respect yourself.

Keep your life free of clutter – Clean your room,

closet, desk, and other important areas that you visit and use every day on your life. A clean and clutter-free surrounding is a crucial element to feeling a sense of freedom and joy within yourself. You feel inexplicably happy in a clean and clutter-free environment. Moreover, cleaning is therapeutic too.

In the same way, clear your mind of clutter and negativity. In fact, when you are clearing out your spaces, make sure you get rid of elements and items that remind you of failed and unhappy relationships/friendships. Consequently, you will find it easy to let go of heavy feelings associated with such unpleasant memories.

Here are some more ways to help you practice self-love on a daily basis:

- Begin each day by affirming self-love. Tell yourself how lovely you look, how well you handled a particularly difficult situation yesterday, how well you did your test last week, or any other positive thing.
- Eat a nutritious and healthy breakfast
- Love and respect your body and treat it well; exercise well and eat well
- Don't believe all your thoughts. Many of the thoughts come in our minds to belittle us.
- Surround yourself with people who love and care for you. Let them remind you how amazing you are.
- Stop comparing yourself with anyone else. You are unique and there is no one like you. Be proud of your uniqueness without being arrogant.
- Avoid all friendships that are toxic in your life. Bullies, people who treat you badly, people who think you are

useless, and all other negative people should be avoided altogether.

- Be proud of all your achievements; big or small
- Understand that beauty is relative and can never have a universal definition.

Maintain a Journal for Confidence

Journaling is one of the most effective ways of building and developing your confidence. Here are some journal prompts that help you build your confidence. Take one prompt at a time and write down your answers:

- What is your best talent?
- List out all the compliments you have received until now. From this, rank what you believe are your top 5
- What do your parents do to build your confidence?
- Write a unique trait that you possess. What makes it so special?
- Write down five statements that describe you. Start with the phrase, 'I am...' Take some time to think about each of the five statements.
- Write an experience in which you did something that you were previously afraid of doing. What were your feelings after that?
- Think of a time when someone, your teacher, your parents, or a sibling, recognized and praised you for something that you worked very hard for. Write down your feelings when the person appreciated your work.
- What are the traits in you that you believe make you a strong person?
- Think of a time when a classmate you are not particularly fond of was struggling with a problem, and you volunteered to help him or her. Write down the

details of that experience and the feelings that came with it.

- Of all the people in your life, who makes you feel the most confident about yourself and why?
- Name three traits about yourself that you love the most.
- Speak to some of your trusted friends, teachers, and family members. Ask them what they think about you. Come back home, and write down these observations in your journal
- Do you believe having confidence is important? If so, why?
- Write down three instances in your life in which you saw other people receive recognition and rewards and wanted to replicate the efforts in your life.

Another reason you need to keep a journal is to make a note of your goals, and keep reading, revising, and updating them as you progress. Journaling helps you revise values, goals, and do daily and weekly evaluations. Also, keep your core values in your journal. Keep evaluating and working on your core values. Knowing the core values right in the beginning itself, rereading them every day and later every week are activities that boost confidence significantly.

More Confidence-Building Tips and Tricks

Have an objective perspective about everything in your life – For example, if you failed a test or didn't get an invitation for a party to which your best friend is invited or did not get admission to the club you wanted to join, then don't jump to any conclusions based on high levels of emotion. Instead, step back from the situation, look at it from all possible perspectives so that you can gather all relevant facts.

Then, perhaps, you can find alternate reasons for the situations mentioned above. For the failed test, the simplest explanation is that one test does not decide your skill or expertise in any subject. Maybe the club you thought was right for you was not really your fit. Maybe your friends thought you were busy studying for an upcoming important exam and didn't want to disturb you.

Give yourself daily credits – At the end of each day, write down the list of things you accomplished that day. Don't worry excessively about how big or small the achievement might have been. Simply write down everything that you did that gave you happiness. Maybe you did a test exceptionally well, or your essay was read out to the entire class because it was written so well that your teacher wanted it to be used as a sample for your classmates to use.

These small goals give you the motivation needed to challenge yourself and work harder the next day to do even better. After you finish listing your achievements for the day, make a list of your next day's goals.

Chapter Summary

In this chapter, you learned more ideas and tips on how to build your confidence levels. You learned the importance and benefits of practicing self-love and self-acceptance to enhance confidence. You also learned how you can use journaling to record and remind yourself of the good qualities you possess. Besides, you learned the importance of keeping an objective perspective to gather facts and arrive at sensible solutions. Lastly, giving yourself daily credits boosts your confidence no end.

Conclusion

Here is a short summary of crucial takeaways from this book on confidence for teenagers:

Confidence is the awareness of one's capabilities minus the expertise-driven arrogance. Confidence can be learned and mastered through practice having confidence has multiple benefits including but not limited to leading a fulfilling and meaningful life and being free from anxieties and fears of inadequacies.

Using the questionnaires and processes given in Chapter 2, you can arrive at your current level of confidence based on which you can plan how to move forward in building and developing this important trait.

A growth mindset and learning and practicing new skills are crucial elements to building confidence. The more skills you learn, the better your confidence level. The journey to confidence-building starts with a decision to begin today with confidence.

Identifying, understanding, and appreciating the importance of core values gives you the required push to begin working on your confidence level. Having a robust set of core values facilitate decision-making and ensuring your life choices are aligned with your core values. Core values guide you to live your life the way you want to.

Identifying and understanding your purpose, mission, and goals of life help you build confidence by keeping you on your chosen path. Goal-setting gives you focus, motivation, and the drive to build a strong value-based and fulfilling life.

Finally, the last three chapters covered various tips, recommendations, and suggestions on how to build your confidence level using affirmations, visualizations, challenging yourself, loving and accepting yourself, and more.

Confidence, self-esteem, and assertiveness are all related and yet different from each other. This part was focused on confidence.

Part 2: Assertiveness for Teens

4 Easy to Use Methods to Stop Bullying
and Stand Up For Yourself

Chapter 1: Types of Communication

Assertiveness is an empowering personality trait that allows you to stand up for your own, and other people's, rights. Assertiveness is congruent with fighting for what is right in a calm and non-aggressive manner. The biggest power of an assertive person is his or her ability to articulate even the most conflicting ideas without upsetting or antagonizing the opposing party.

The quality of assertiveness is to stand up firmly for your rights by expressing your feelings, thoughts, and beliefs in honest, direct, and non-aggressive ways. It is important to note that assertiveness includes deep sensitivity for the thoughts, beliefs, and feelings of other people. Assertiveness is typically seen as a balance between passive and aggressive behaviors.

Since assertiveness is connected to communication and behaviors, it will help to know the different communication styles that exist to improve the understanding of assertiveness better. Here are the primary types of communication:

1. Passive
2. Aggressive
3. Assertive
4. Passive-Aggressive

Let us look at each type in a little detail, along with some examples.

Passive Communication

People with a passive style of communication tend not to express their feelings, opinion, and thoughts openly. They are not equipped to fight for their rights. Passive communication is typically associated with low self-esteem. Based on their belief that they are not worth taking care of, passive communicators do not respond overtly to angry or hurtful situations.

Instead, they unwittingly accumulate negative feelings and resentment. But, one can only collect and hold so much negativity. Therefore, such people are prone to emotional outbursts when their threshold levels are breached.

Passive Communicators:
- Do not assert themselves even when they know they should
- Allow others to infringe on their rights
- Do not express their opinions and needs
- Nearly always speak in an apologetic tone
- Exhibit slumped body posture and do not maintain eye contact

All these actions or inactions result in feelings of

depression, inadequacy, immaturity, and confusions. Passive communication is good at times, especially when you are required to show deference to people better qualified and more knowledgeable than you. However, if it is your default mode of communication, then silence is not golden.

Examples of How a Passive Communicator Would Talk and Behave:

- I am not able to fight off that bully
- I am not smart enough to clear the test
- I am not worthy of being in the school basketball team
- None of my friends care for me

Challenges of Passive Communication:

- People will disregard your needs and opinions
- You will easily be passed up for promotions and other good offers
- You will build unnecessary stress
- You expect others to be able to read your mind
- Can lead to an aggressive communication style in a very dangerous way
- You will most likely end up being a bully or a bully's side-kick

Have you ever heard of great leaders of the world who have this style of communication? Never!

Aggressive Communication

If passive communicators are at one end of the communication spectrum, then aggressive communicators are at the opposite end. Aggressive communicators express their opinions and feelings so strongly that it violates the rights of others around them.

Aggressive Communicators:

- Dominate others
- Humiliate people to control them
- Attack, criticize, and blame others
- Speak in demanding and loud voices
- Act rudely or threateningly
- Are bad listeners
- Are frequent interrupters
- Maintain an overbearing posture and piercing eye contact

Examples of How Aggressive Communicators Talk and Behave:

- I am right, and you are wrong
- I am superior to you
- I can infringe upon your rights
- I will get my way, no matter what
- Everything is your fault
- You owe me

Challenges of Aggressive Communicators:

If you are a default aggressive communicator, you are going to be:

- Alienated by your friends and peers
- No one will want to be identified with you
- You will generate hatred and fear among your friends; consequently, you will remain friendless
- You will always find external circumstances and other people to blame for your failures, because of which you will never be able to grow and mature

Aggressive leaders from history have always been referred to as ruthless. Here are a few classic examples:

Genghis Khan – Although he is credited with uniting the Mongol tribes into a powerful single country which succeeded in conquering nearly the whole of China, his methods are considered brutal. He is known to have slaughtered and plundered civilians thoughtlessly and ruthlessly.

Queen Mary I – Also referred to as Bloody Mary, she was the only child of King Henry VIII and Catherine of Aragon. In an attempt to restore Catholicism in England, she gave orders to burn hundreds of Protestants at the stake.

Joseph Stalin – To bring about rapid collectivization and industrialization in the 1930s in the USSR, Stalin imprisoned millions of workers in labor camps, starved them, carried out the 'Great Purge' of the intelligentsia, armed forces, and the government in his country.

A common denominator of such aggressive leaders is the fact that they were willing to do anything to achieve what they believed was right with utter disregard for everyone and everything else.

Passive-Aggressive Communication

People who have developed the passive-aggressive style of communication seem passive on the surface but are, in truth, showing anger subtly and indirectly.

Have you seen Prisoners-of-War (POWs) behaving in movies? Most of them are characterized as showing this behavior because of the overwhelming feeling of helplessness combined with simmering rage. POWs are often characterized by the way they mock the enemy or indulge in some behind-the-scene act of sabotage.

Alternatively, how have you behaved with your parents when they try to discipline? Muttering something nasty under your breath while following their instructions half-heartedly? That is another example of passive-aggressive communication.

Passive-Aggressive Communicators:

- Mutter under their breath instead of confronting the issue or person
- Do not acknowledge their anger openly
- Their body language and their feelings are mismatched; they could be smiling when they are actually angry
- Employ sarcasm frequently
- Appear to cooperate but try to sabotage in an underhanded way

Examples of How Passive-Aggressive Communicators Talk and Behave:

- I frustrate and sabotage because I am weak and helpless
- I do not know how to beat your scores through hard work and so I will find ways to cheat and get better scores
- I will look as if I am cooperating, but I resent the

situation I am in

Challenges of Passive-Aggressive Communicators:
- They remain stuck in positions of helplessness, just like the POWs
- They will be able to vent off resentment through stealth, although real issues never get addressed
- They become alienated from people around them

Examples of Passive-Aggressive Behaviors in School:
The teacher has given orders to sit quietly and work out 10 Math problems. There will typically be at least a few students who will do everything but sit silently at their desks. They could be performing seemingly innocuous tasks, such as sharpening their pencils with the needless ruckus, rubbing their eyes and yawning loudly, asking for a restroom break, or some such thing.

Students deliberately underperform to exhibit their passive-aggressive behavior to their teachers. They will scribble their assignments and make it impossible for their teacher to read and grade them. They will deliberately give wrong answers, despite knowing the right ones.

Assertive Communication

Assertive communication is one in which people clearly state and express their opinions and needs without hurting or violating the rights of other people. They are firm and yet do not exhibit aggression of any sort.

Malala Yousufzai, a Pakistani activist for women's education, became the youngest Nobel Prize laureate when she won the Nobel Peace Prize in 2014. She literally challenged and overcame the fear of death to stand up to for her right to education, even as she was shot and left for dead by terrorists. She said, "I raised my voice not so that I can shout but so that people without a voice can be heard."

Millie Bobby Brown is a teenage sensation who plays the role of a mysterious girl in the famous sci-fi series, Stranger Things. She says, "I am a strong person. Even if people say something horrible about me, I just respond with, 'Ok, whatever,' and continue being me."

Assertiveness is closely related to high self-esteem.

Assertive Communicators:
- Express their needs and opinions appropriately, clearly, and respectfully
- Take responsibility for their actions
- Communicate with everyone with dignity and respect
- Are in control of their emotions
- Speak in a calm and relaxed tone of voice
- Maintain a relaxed body posture
- Are competent and in control of the situation
- Do not allow people to manipulate and abuse them
- Stand up firmly for their rights

Examples of How Assertive Communicators Talk and Behave:
- We are all equally entitled to our rights, opinions, and feelings
- I am confident of myself
- I know that I have choices in my life, and I must weigh

the pros and cons and make the correct choices for my life
- I speak honestly and clearly
- I don't beat around the bush; I state my case to the point
- I will stand up for my rights and will not allow them to be violated by anyone
- I respect and honor the rights of other people

Effects of Being an Assertive Communicator:
- You will be respected by your friends and peers
- You will address core issues in your life, which will help you to grow and mature as an individual.
- As you create a friendly environment to include everyone, you will always be well-liked and popular

Nearly every great leader of the world has been able to exhibit his or her assertiveness. Here are some classic examples, whose behaviors you can emulate right from your teenage years, which will hold you in good stead all through your life:

Abraham Lincoln – Known for his calm and composed demeanor, Abraham Lincoln was an amazing communicator who never offended anyone with his superiority. He was basically a quiet man except when the need to stand up for rights was there. Then, he would stand tall and firm, and fight openly, honestly, and without violating the rights of others.

Rosa Parks – This civil rights movement leader was the epitome of quiet assertiveness. Although not very outspoken, she did not hesitate to do what was right, even in the face of hostility.

Assertiveness helps us take care of ourselves and our needs and is an essential ingredient for a happy and healthy life. There is a general acceptance that men are naturally more assertive than women. This general outlook enhances the pressure on both girls and boys to learn and master assertiveness for the following reason:

- Girls – because they have to work harder than boys to become assertive
- Boys – because they have to live up to the standards expected by society

The good thing about assertiveness is that it can be imbibed by anyone with a little practice, patience, and diligence. In fact, those who don't try to learn the art of assertiveness will be at a big disadvantage in today's highly competitive world.

Chapter 2: Why Do We Behave the Way We Do?

Why do people behave the way they do? What drives them? Why are some people aggressive to the point of hurting others while others are passive-aggressive and pretend to do one thing while wanting the exact opposite? In modern culture, we are conditioned to believe that suppressing or not expressing your feelings and emotions is the best way to handle them.

Nothing can be farther from the truth considering that emotions, along with intellect and other mechanisms, are used by us to understand what is happening to us and around us. In fact, emotions give us the energy to come to terms with the various ups and downs in our lives.

The human body works best when it is in homeostasis, which is a balanced state. When we inhale, we are out of balance, and when we exhale, the balanced state is restored. Similarly, our mind goes out of balance when emotions find their way into our system, and unless there is an exit for those feelings, we continue to remain in an unbalanced state. Our system cannot be in a state of homeostasis if these emotions are not discharged from our body completely without leaving trace remnants too.

Expressing our feelings is the best form of exit for our emotions. If we continue to allow our feelings to accumulate inside us instead of expressing them, they will build pressure in our system, which is called the 'percolator effect' in psychology. A percolator is an old-fashioned coffee-brewing machine which builds pressure inside through heating so that coffee is brewed.

Similarly, if emotions, which are nothing but forms of energy, are not released, the pressure inside you is going to build up. When it crosses a certain threshold (which is dependent on the individual's capability to hold such pressures), it will burst forth in nasty ways, including in the form of physical pain such as stomachache, gastritis, ulcers, etc. Of course, the most common way of expressing such repressed emotions is to demonstrate it on family and loved ones by screaming, yelling, and even physical abuse.

While some people bring out repression in aggressive ways, others use passive-aggressive methods. As discussed in Chapter 1, aggressive behavior takes on the form of physical abuse, yelling, and screaming; passive-aggressive behavior comes in the form of cursing under the breath, deliberately underperforming, etc.

So, every time you get angry or frustrated or upset about something and you don't find a healthy way to engage with these emotions and release the energy from your system, the emotional pressure is bound to build and end up in nasty situations for you. While your aggressive behavior has bad outcomes for the victim, it results in even worse results for you.

Let us look at some of the reasons, along with examples of aggressive and passive-aggressive behavior. Many times, the causes for your negative emotions might be beyond your control; however, you must remember how you respond to these problems is entirely in your control.

Reasons for Aggressive and Passive-Aggressive Behaviors in Teenagers

Numerous studies have been conducted and multiple reasons have emerged as to why teenagers behave aggressively. Some of the reasons include:

Trauma – Illness or death of a loved one, extreme harassment by parents or siblings, ongoing discords and fights between parents or divorce are all highly stressful situations. Teenagers are not mature enough to handle such pressures well. Instead, they become aggressive.

Ingrid Bergman, one of the most captivating stars of Hollywood, had a very troubled childhood. Her mother died when she was 3 years old, and her father died when she was a teenager. She was forced to live with an uncle who was against her wanting to become an actress. A classic case for aggressive behavior! And yet, she rose above the challenges and became one of the most exotic actresses the world has ever seen.

Abuse – Sexual, mental, or physical abuse is another common reason for aggressive behavior amongst teenagers. The abuse angers the children, and yet they feel helpless against older and stronger people. It is also not easy to find someone trusting to talk about such things with. So, their emotions pile up inside and aggression is their way out.

Rita Hayworth, the famous glamorous actress and dancer of the 20th century, had a very troubled adolescence because of her extremely demanding father. He pushed her unreasonably hard to achieve success. While she did achieve success, her adolescence is sure to have been very, very difficult.

Peer Pressure – Puberty is a very difficult time for most teenagers. Raging hormones wreak havoc on the body and mind. Weight gain, freckles, and other forms of physical awkwardness make teenagers the butt of jokes and victims of bullying. Sometimes, wanting to belong and being rejected creates stress for young people. Such situations also drive aggressive behavior.

Janis Joplin is, perhaps, one of the most famous and popular rock stars of the 20th century. Her most turbulent period was her teenage years. Puberty kicked in and she gained weight. She was the butt of all ridicule and humiliation in school and among her peers. She had to fight her way out of it. It was only when Janis came into contact with like-minded people who shared her interest in music and singing that she found her peace with life.

Of course, after that, there was nothing to stop her growth.

Addiction and Abuse – Adolescence is a very vulnerable age. Peer pressure and the desire to 'fit in' drives many teenagers to try drugs and alcohol. After a certain point, many of them become addicted to these items, and aggression is one of the most common negative effects of addiction.

Low Self-Esteem – This is, perhaps, one of the most important reasons for teenagers becoming aggressive. Many teenagers are victims of low self-esteem due to multiple reasons, including emotional conflicts, stressful academic pressures, high parental expectations, and more. They exhibit aggressive behavior to cover up their low self-esteem.

Don't panic if you are a teenager showing aggressive behavior. The good thing about aggressive behavior in teenagers is that it is very easy to manage and overcome because you are still young, and you have time and energy on your side to learn to become masters of your emotions instead of being under control of your feelings.

Examples of Aggressive Teenagers Who Turned Out Really Well in Adult Life

Jay Z – This famous musician, rapper, and producer was arrested when he was 16 for carrying crack. A very inspiring quote from him: "The way to redemption is not to run away from your error-ridden past but to understand and learn from the mistakes and build a strong future."

Charles Sutton – This famous actor was arrested and convicted for manslaughter when he was 17. He even attacked a guard in jail. He turned around when he found a purpose in his life: to become an actor. He says, "I used to be a hard-hearted person. However, once I decided to change, many good things started happening."

Dwayne Johnson – This successful wrestler with a highly successful film career admitted to being arrested 8 or 9 times by the time he was 16. Today, he only remembers thinking of a firm resolution he made to himself the last time he was arrested: that he would do everything in his power not to let it happen in his life again.

Stephen Fry – One of Britain's biggest stars of all times, Stephen Fry was arrested for credit card fraud when he was 17. His life turned around after he completed his sentencing. This man returned to college and devoted himself entirely to his studies. In his autobiography, Stephen Fry says, "I used to feel the working of my heart and lungs thumping energy through my entire body. I felt the enormity of real, human power I possessed; the power to strive and endure continuously."

Some Interesting Pointers to Passive-Aggressive Behaviors

Why do some people use passive aggression instead of direct aggression? Please remember that the effects and outcomes of both behaviors are the same; emotions are not handled effectively and healthily in both cases. Yet, passive aggression is seen more commonly than direct aggression. Here are a few reasons for that:

Direct anger is not whereas sugar-coated anger is accepted in society – We have always been taught to hide anger because it is a socially unaccepted emotion.

However, you are allowed to put up a fight in a 'nice sugar-coated' way. So, we put on a show of not being angry by using subversive means of releasing the emotion through underhand dealings, or muttering under our breath or seeking revenge indirectly, etc.

It is easy to rationalize passive-aggression – For example, suppose your dad told you to clean your room. You get angry first, then you pout, then you procrastinate, and finally, on repeated persistence, you simply take everything lying around in your room and shove it under your bed. Now, your dad is furious. You quickly rationalize by saying, "I don't see why you're so angry. I was planning to clean up after studying for my exams." Alternatively, you might say, "No matter what I do, you always find fault." And your poor dad does not know how to respond.

See how easy it is to rationalize passive-aggression and put the other person on the defensive?

Revenge is sweet – Passive aggression is all about taking revenge in a round-about way, and revenge is undoubtedly sweet; all the more if the avenger gets it with social acceptance! You are tired after a hectic day at school, and you want your father to stop nagging (or so you think) you about cleaning your room. So, you shove everything under the bed knowing very well he is going to fume! That look of helpless rage when you gave that almost perfect but hollow excuse of wanting to clean it after studying for your exams was sweet, wasn't it?

Regardless of these reasons, passive aggression is not an effective way of handling and releasing emotional energy.

The most effective way of handling emotion is through assertiveness; letting people know your opinions and emotions in a firm but gentle way without hurting other people's feelings.

Chapter 3: Current Level of Assertiveness

Let us start by gauging your current level of assertiveness with a simple questionnaire based on a self-expression scale taken from the academic literature produced under the title The College Self-Expression Scale (by John P. Galassi & others) published in 1974.

Questionnaire to Gauge the Current Level of Assertiveness for Teenagers

These questions are worded to prompt a 'yes' or a 'no' answer from you. At the end of it, you will be able to see what level of assertiveness you are at, and which areas you need to improve on. The more Yeses, the more assertive you are.

Q1. Suppose you are standing in line along with 10 other students to submit an application form at the school office. Now, someone new comes and goes straight to the office to hand over his or her application form without even glancing at the line of students patiently waiting to do the same thing. Will you raise your voice? Y/N

Q2. You shopped for a pair of sneakers at a big departmental store located quite a distance away from your home. When you came home, you realized they were slightly defective. Will you take the trouble to go back and get them exchanged? Y/N

Q3. You had a huge argument with your friend regarding a particular assignment to be done jointly with her or him. The friend finally gave in to your argument, and both of you submitted it the way you insisted over your friend's suggestion. However, your teacher returned it, asking that the assignment be redone in precisely the same way your friend had suggested. Will you apologize to your friend for your mistake? Y/N

Q4. If you are angry with your parents for any reason, do you always tell them in an honest and upfront way about your feelings, along with the reasons for the anger? Y/N

Q5. Your best friend borrowed some money from you about a month ago saying he would return it to you when he received his next pocket money. You know that his parents have already given him his pocket money. Will you remind him to return your money? Y/N

Q6. When you are talking to other people including friends, teachers, and family members, are you sensitive to their feelings when you respond to them or discuss things that you know will affect their emotions? Y/N

Q7. Continuing from Q6, do you make an effort to say what you
have to say without hurting them but without being overly

sensitive to their feelings? Y/N

Q8. If you need a favor from a friend, do you ask for it openly without feeling uncomfortable? Y/N

Q9. You are on your first date with a boy/girl whom you worked very hard to get. The dinner at the restaurant is not to their satisfaction. Will you let the waiter know your feelings, even at the risk of coming across as picky and choosy in front of your date? Y/N

Q10. You walk into a garment shop, and you simply love the red dress on the mannequin. The salesman also says wonderful things about the dress. However, you know it is very pricey and you cannot afford it. Would you stand your ground and say no to the salesman and not feel uncomfortable about it? Y/N

Q11. You are studying for an upcoming important exam. Suddenly a group of friends drop in to chat and generally chill out with you. Will you politely tell them to return at a more convenient time? Y/N

Q12. Do you feel comfortable sharing opinions with your peers and siblings?

Q13. Do you feel comfortable sharing opinions with your parents?

Q14. Do you feel comfortable sharing opinions with your teachers and other elders in your life?

Q15. You are in a history class. History is your favorite subject, and the teacher is your favorite too. The teacher suddenly says something that you know to be incorrect. Will you stand up and correct the teacher? Y/N

Q16. Your dad's boss, whom you have met before and are very fond of, comes home to dinner one day and says something that you strongly disagree with. Will you make an effort to present the countering viewpoint?

Q17. You went to a store and bought something and walked out. On the way home you realize that you were short-changed. Would you walk back and request to be given the right amount back? Y/N

Q18. A really good friend, from whom you have taken help to do your Math assignments because you are weak in the subject, comes to you with an unreasonable request. Will you be able to refuse politely? Y/N

Q19. One of your most loved uncles is behaving in a very annoying way recently. Will you find a way to tell him politely that his behavior is not nice? Y/N

Q20. Suppose you are playing a game with some junior players. You and your friend are experts at this particular sport. However, the junior players are very skilled, and it looks like they are going to win the match. Suddenly you notice your friend sneakily indulging in a cheating act, which will result in you winning the match. Will you own up to what happened and concede defeat? Y/N

Q21. You shared a very deep secret with your best friend, and he betrays your confidence by spreading the secret around. He is not only your best friend but also a very popular guy at school. Will you stand up and tell him you are disappointed with him and want nothing to do with him anymore? Y/N

Q22. You are standing in line at a departmental store to bill the items you have purchased. The billing clerk attends to a person who came after you. Will you bring this unfair act to the attention of the store manager? Y/N

Q23. You desperately need some money. Are you comfortable asking your friend to help? Y/N

Q24. You are a fairly good sport and can take jokes on yourself quite well. However, a good friend has gone a bit overboard teasing you, and you are not feeling nice about it. Will you stand up and tell your friend your feelings? Y/N

Q25. You have arrived late for an important meeting. Will you have the courage to walk up to the front row and take a seat, even if this action draws attention to you? Before answering, remember you have the option of sitting inconspicuously at the back. Y/N

Q26. You are engaged in a conversation with a friend, and an important person (perhaps, someone of good social standing) interrupts your conversation. Will you tell the person to excuse you until you finish the current conversation? Y/N

Q27. Someone is unjustly finding fault with you. Can you tactfully express your disagreement? Y/N

Q28. Do you believe you are comfortable being assertive? Y/N

Look at the 'No' answers, and explore the situation again, and see what it takes for you to reconsider the answer. Do you need to reprogram your thinking process to make yourself more assertive in the given situation? What are the causes of your behavior? Can you connect anything personal to that particular behavior which is preventing you from being assertive? What changes can you bring about in yourself to be more assertive?

Maintain an Assertiveness Journal

For about two weeks, maintain an assertiveness journal in which you make daily entries. Note down each incident when you could have shown assertiveness. It could be discussions, unfair practice, bullying, someone cheating in a test, or anything else. Make a note of the following elements:

- Did you voice your opinion?
- How did you talk?
- What were the emotions going through your mind?
- Did you think you managed the emotions easily enough and remained calm and composed, or were you struggling?
- Did your ability to manage your emotions affect the result? If yes, how?
- Did you believe you could have handled the discussion in a better way? Were you happy with the outcome or was the other party happy? Did you dwell excessively on the outcome of the discussion?

These are only pointers. Make a note of all the relevant

things that you know affected the outcome. Don't judge yourself while making the entries. Remember you are in the process of learning. Now, at the end of two weeks, read through your journal and see if you can pick out triggers that drove your behavior in any particular way. Can you see a pattern in your behavior?

If you are unsure of making objective observations, show your journal to a trusted friend, and discuss with him or her openly and honestly. You can arrive at your current level of assertiveness using the information from these diary entries.

Get to Know Your Current Communication Style

Choose the most appropriate answer that matches your current communication level. Be honest. Otherwise, there is no value in this exercise. Everyone is struggling to improve themselves.

Q1. Someone gets ahead of you while you are in line. What do you do?
1. Give them the benefit of the doubt and tell them gently that you were waiting before them
2. Glare at them angrily while saying nothing, and push them 'accidentally' to take your rightful place
3. Say and do nothing
4. Express your displeasure firmly and tell them to go back to their place

Q2. You are meeting your friend to do your class project

together. You came on time, and your friend arrived nearly 30 minutes late. What do you do?

1. You rudely tell your friend you don't like to be kept waiting for so long
2. Say nothing because you don't like conflict
3. Look at your watch, and ask your friend for an explanation for the delay
4. Say nothing because you left after waiting for 10 minutes

Q3. Your friend constantly makes you the butt of all his jokes in class. You have already told him that his attitude hurts you. But he has not relented. What do you do?

1. Decide to build a thicker skin so that you don't feel bad about these jokes
2. Re-evaluate the value of this friendship in your life, and do the needful to get out
3. Start making your friend the butt of your own jokes, matching each joke of his with your own veiled attack
4. Don't talk about jokes again, but bring up topics that you know anger and annoy your friend

Gauging your current level of assertiveness arms you with the relevant information needed to take corrective measures in building and strengthening your assertiveness level.

Chapter 4: Building Assertiveness Based on Your Core Values

Core or personal values are qualities or traits that you don't just consider worthwhile, but which form the fundamental driving force of your life. Personal core values guide your life choices and your behaviors. If you get your core values right, then you will be able to make swift and focused decisions that are aligned with your life purpose.

The Elements that Define Core Values

There are primarily three elements that define core values, including:

1. ***Theoretically, you should be able to live by them irrespective of your physical condition*** – For example, honesty is a core value that can be lived by you no matter where you are. You could be stuck in a little prison cell, and even then remain honest. However, if your core value was physical fitness, then it might not be possible to live by it at all times and in all places. Therefore, being athletic or being physically fit cannot

101

really be a core value.

2. ***There is no need for participation or approval from anyone else but you*** – The entire world could turn against you. But you should still be able to live by your chosen core value. For example, if courage is a core value, then you don't need anyone's approval or participation to be courageous. However, popularity requires the approval and participation of other people. Therefore, courage can be a core value whereas popularity cannot.

3. ***You should be able to apply them internally and externally simultaneously*** – This means you should be able to live by and act on the core value for yourself and for those around you together without sacrificing anyone, including yourself. This point is best explained with an illustration. For example, being a martyr cannot be a valued principle or behavior because hurting yourself for the sake of others means you are not being compassionate to yourself.

Importance of Core Values

Your core values help you choose your relationships, your friendships, your career path, and more. Core values help you manage your energy, time, and money resources sensibly and wisely. You can focus the use of these resources productively in the direction of your core values.

Your core values give you a personal code of conduct, which helps you stay on your chosen life path even in the face of adversity. When you consistently honor your core values, you are bound to achieve a sense of fulfillment. If you don't have a set of core values, or fail to follow one that you have given yourself, you are likely to fall into bad habits and regress into behaviors that are misaligned with your life purpose. When you realize your personal core values, your behavior undergoes change.

And finally, core values are very important to build your level of assertiveness. They are the guiding factors that tell you when to stand your ground, and when it is okay to let go. Core values help you with the following:

Help you make good decisions - Core values become the basis of your decision-making. They guide you to make the right choices. The absence of core values will make you uncertain about the choices you make and make you feel less assertive than required.

Help you remain confident and centered – Doing the 'right' thing will be easy if you don't have an overreaching set of guiding principles in the form of your core values. Core values help you analyze facts, emotions, and circumstances, upon which you can do the 'right' thing on a consistent basis which, in turn, builds confidence while keeping you grounded and centered.

Identifying your core values, therefore, is the cornerstone of building and growing your assertiveness.

Discovering Your Core Values

As a teenager, it is quite likely that you still haven't formed your core values. Here are some steps to help you personalize your values for yourself:

Firstly, create a list of personal values. There are more than 400 values that you can choose from, including love, acceptance, justice, temperance, prudence, ambition, friendship, respect, fun, health, responsibility, balance, health, and lots, lots more.

However, avoid going by any pre-determined list of core values. Core values make sense when you discover them from your life experiences instead of inventing them from a list constructed by someone else. Here are some pointers to help you discover your core values:

Recall your peak experiences – Think back to a moment in your life when your experience felt truly meaningful. A peak experience is something we don't ever forget. Spend some time to list 2-3 such experiences in your life. Answer the following questions regarding those experiences:

- Describe the event or experience.
- What were the feelings in your mind?
- What was going on in your mind?
- What were the values that you were committing to yourself at that time? It could have been unwitting at that time. However, now when you recall those experiences, those values will stand out.

Recall your worst experiences – Now, in the same way, recall a couple of the worst experiences, and as above, write down answers to the same set of questions, except the last question will be: "What were the values that you were suppressing?"

Define your code of conduct – After your basic human needs including food, clothing, and shelter are met, what are the next most important elements of life that you must necessarily have to achieve fulfillment and make your life meaningful. Here are some examples:

- A sense of adventure and excitement
- Creativity
- Health and vitality
- Learning new things
- Beauty of nature

Primarily, what are those personal values without which your life simply withers away? Or what are those personal values without which you might live but never thrive?

Combine similar values together from your list – Take the list of values you get from the above experiences and categorize similar values together if the list is long and unwieldy. For example, timeliness, accountability, and responsibility can be clubbed together. Development, learning, and growth can all be combined.

Identify the theme of each group of values – For example, timeliness, accountability, and responsibility can be grouped as discipline and development; learning, and growth can be categorized as learning and growth.

Take the top 5 from this set of core values – Again, if you are still left with a big list, take the top 4-5 core values that are essential for life. Use your answers to the following questions to help you:

- What values are absolutely necessary for your life?

- What values reflect your life path?
- What values are needed to be content and happy?

Ideally, the number of your core values should be somewhere between 5 and 10. If it is less, then you could risk leaving out critical elements of your life. If the list of your core values is very long, remembering and keeping track of them might prove to be difficult.

And finally, rank your core values in order of importance. This last step could be the most challenging part of setting up your core values. Take some time and do your ranking. Sleep on it and recheck to see if you have conflicts. Rearrange the ranking if required. Persist until you are completely sure of your core values and their order of importance in your life.

At this point, it makes sense to list some examples of ideas and concepts that cannot be used as core values because they don't meet one or more of the 3-element criteria mentioned above:

- Family connection – this core requires the participation of other people
- Financial security – this also requires favorable factors beyond your control
- Marriage – again, a partner's participation and approval is required
- Physical fitness or strength – this requires comparison with others, a particular physical situation, for it to be effective
- Emotional detachment – this also requires societal approval as to what is considered emotional

detachment; moreover, external circumstances beyond your control could easily prevent you from living by this principle

- Travel – requires money, time, and other external resources

Core Values and Assertiveness

Once you have your core values in place and are completely engaged with it, your ability to enhance your level of assertiveness will go up a few notches.

Chapter 5: Change Your Inner Beliefs

One of the most significant challenges to increasing your assertiveness level is your own thinking. All of us are molded by conditions and thinking processes that have been ingrained in us from our childhood. As a teenager, some of your thought processes are already deeply cemented in your mind. For example, you have pre-existing thoughts about yourself, the people around you, and the world at large.

Many times, these beliefs and pre-set thoughts are a result

of our own experiences, along with what has been taught to us by our parents, teachers, friends, etc. For instance, as a child you were taught not to show negative emotions, such as anger and sadness, because you would be mocked.

This attitude might have made sense then because it was an effective way to quieten a bawling kid. However, now as a teenager, you don't need to work within the same parameters. It is perfectly alright to express negative emotions because you are now old enough to keep your feelings and expressions in reasonable check. And yet, controlled by those archaic conditions, we are still scared or disinclined to express negative emotions.

Changing Your Mindset that Facilitates Assertive Behavior

Now, as a teenager, you have to tell your mind to unlearn old and archaic conditionings and learn and master new thoughts and inner beliefs that facilitate assertive behavior. Here are some examples:

1. Staying silent works like cancer and is a trait of a coward. There is no wisdom in not standing up for your rights, opinions, and feelings. By standing up for your rights, you might not win every battle you participate in. But, everyone will know what you stood for – so said Shannon L. Adler. She is an inspirational author who has multiple bestselling books to her credit.

   Therefore, don't stagnate in old valueless beliefs that are not relevant anymore. Allow your heart and mind to grow and evolve as you pass each stage of your life.

Be ready to eliminate irrelevant and limiting beliefs and embrace new and forward-thinking concepts and ideas.

2. Warren Buffet, one of the most successful businessmen and global business investor of all times, says, "The primary difference between truly successful and ordinarily successful people is that the truly successful people say NO to most of the things."

Gauge your current mindset and inner belief. Understand where you are presently and where you want to reach. Once you are clear about your purpose and core values of your life, then focus on only those things that add value to these important elements. Channelize all your energies towards this goal alone and stay away from or say NO to everything else.

For example, if your 4-year life purpose is to complete a computer science engineering course, then your entire teenage life should be focused on this target alone. Let all your energies and resources be channelized towards this one goal and change your mindset completely for this purpose. For everything else, the answer is NO.

3. Malcolm X, the American Muslim minister and human rights activist, said, "No one can give you equality, freedom, justice, or anything else. If you are man enough, then reach out and take it."

Until you take things into your own hands and do what is needed to get justice and freedom, these elements will always be beyond your reach. As a child, many things in your life were done for you by your parents and caretakers. However, think back and you will recollect and, slowly but surely, your parents would have handed over the responsibility of things for yourself.

For example, there was a time when you literally needed to be spoon-fed. Soon, you learned to assert yourself to eat on your own. In fact, ask your parents and they will tell you that you fought to eat on your own. It is an innate survival behavior to be aggressive. Our ancestors had to be aggressive to survive.

However, as we learned to civilize ourselves, we picked up the skill of toning our aggression down to assertiveness because modern life does not need aggression. It only requires us to politely view our thoughts without infringing upon the freedom of others to view their own.

Driven by several factors (as discussed in Chapter 2), some of us retained the original aggressive spirit while others turned to passiveness or a passive-aggression style of communication. Assertiveness calls for a healthy balance between passiveness and aggression and balancing it is always a difficult thing to achieve.

Assertiveness, therefore, requires you to look within yourself, and change your mindset and inner beliefs, which will then be reflected in your outward behavior and lifestyle.

How to Gauge Your Current Inner Beliefs

Making changes or moving forward calls for you to understand the current status. Therefore, the first thing you must to do to change yourself is identify your present state regarding inner beliefs. Here are some ways to help you:

Maintain thought diaries – Thoughts run amok in our heads, and remembering them is a huge challenge. Writing them down is the best way to handle this challenge. Start maintaining a diary for your unassertive thoughts, behaviors, and emotions, all of which are driven by your inner beliefs. Here is an example of entries in your thought diary, from which you can write your own journal.

Identifying emotions - Suppose you asked a friend to go with you to a party, and she said, 'No.' Dig deep into your mind and find answers to the following questions:
- What emotions did you feel?
- What was the intensity of these emotions (rate them as per your own ranking system; a classic example is from 1-10 in which 1 stands for 'least intense' and 10 stands for 'most intense.')

Identifying behavior - In this situation where you were hurt and annoyed, how did you behave? Answer the following questions:
- What did you do?
- What were the physical sensations and how intense were they?

Identifying thoughts –You felt tense, worried, and anxious. Identify your thoughts by answering the following

questions:
- What were your thoughts?
- What was running through your head? Rate the intensity of these thoughts?
  Some ground rules while you are answering these questions:
- Stick to facts
- Don't add your interpretations of the situation. For example: "She was rude to me," should not be an entry in your diary
- Rate the intensity of your emotions, thoughts, and physical sensations in each of these situations (the higher the intensity, the more the strength of your inner belief)

Making entries in your diary as mentioned above is the first part of this exercise. The second part consists of rating the strength of your beliefs. The higher the intensity of your thoughts, emotions, and behavior, the stronger your inner belief based on which these elements were triggered should be. Now, answer the following questions for the second part of the diary:
- Were my reactions and responses passive, aggressive, passive-aggressive or assertive?
- What was the evidence of my thoughts, emotions, and behaviors?
- Was I ignoring my rights and opinions or was I ignoring the other person involved in the situation?
- What were the other perspectives of the situation that I was missing?

As you answer these questions, you will get insights into

how you could have been more assertive. Moreover, you also get a clear idea of what your inner beliefs are, from which you can work towards moving in a direction more conducive to an assertive way of thinking and living.

Here is a template for the first situation, when you asked your friend to go to a party:

Part I of the Thought Diary:
What emotions was I feeling? – Angry – 8 (the rating), hurt – 7
Physical sensations – Tight chest, tears in my eyes, tense, angry when I thought of my friend

What did I do? – Punched the boxing bag, cried a bit, and did not pick up her next call

What were my thoughts? – When she asked me to come to a party I didn't want to go, I went for her. She should have done the same for me. I don't think she wants to be my friend.

Intensity of these thoughts – 8

What kind of reactions are these? – Passive, because I didn't have the courage to present my feelings to her. Aggressive, when I punched the boxing bag. Passive-aggressive when I ignored her call.

Part II of the Thought Diary:

Was there any evidence that my thoughts and emotions were true? – No

113

Was there evidence that my thoughts and emotions could have been false? – Yes, she has done a lot of things in the past for me

Did I ignore anyone's rights? – Yes, I ignored my rights when I said yes to her request to go to a party when I didn't want to go. I ignored her rights when she chose to say no to me. The right I ignored is that everyone has a right to say no

Were there other perspectives that I could have missed in this situation? – Yes, she could have been tired. She might have had something really important to do which compelled her to say no to me. There were many occasions when I have also said no to her.

What could have been a more assertive kind of thinking in this situation? – My acceptance that she has a right to say no, and that her denial does not affect our relationship in any way.

What could have been a more assertive way of thinking in this situation? – I could have suggested a raincheck.

After this, rerate your emotions: Hurt – 2, Anger – 2
Use this template to create entries in your thought diary. Keep at this endeavor until you have been able to alter your inner beliefs significantly.

Chapter 6: Communication Techniques to Practice

So, what are the communication techniques that you should practice to increase your level of assertiveness? Before we go into the details of assertive communication, let us understand the reason why everyone is not equally assertive.

Factors that influence people to communicate passively:
- Lack of self-confidence
- Excessively focused on pleasing others
- Excessively worried that their ideas and opinions will not be accepted by others
- Sensitive to criticism
- Not working on assertive communication skills
  Factors that influence people to communicate aggressively:
- Overconfidence
- Focusing excessively on getting their own needs and desires fulfilled
- Not learning to consider and respect other people's opinions, needs, and ideas
- Insufficient listening skills

Factors that influence people to communicate assertively:

- The right level of self-confidence and awareness of their own strengths and weaknesses
- Knowing that their opinions, views, and ideas, as well as those of others, matter equally
- Resilience to criticism, rejections, and other failures

Tips to Improve Assertive Communication

Use these all-purpose assertive phrases and sentences that work very well in most situations:

- Thank you for your time, but I am not interested.
- Thank you very much, but I'm afraid I cannot make time for that now.
- Thank you for your offer, but I need some me-time for the moment.
- Thanks, but no (accompanied by a genuine smile)
- Thank you for including me in this program, but I'm sorry, I will have to pass that up this time
- Thank you for connecting with me, but there is something more important that needs my attention right now.
- Thank you for sharing your opinion. What does the rest of the group think?
- I appreciate your love for partying. But, that really is not my cup of tea.
- That does sound good. Can I take some time to think over it?
- I am not sure right now. Can I take a couple of weeks to ponder over your request?

117

- This sounds very important. But I am unable to give the required attention right now. Can we discuss this thing in, say, a week's time?
- I don't appreciate your words (or tone of voice or below-the-belt comment)
- I truly appreciate your interest in my case.
- I don't agree with your perspective. This is how I see it.
- Please appreciate (or respect) my perspective too.
- I am offended by what you said.

Learn some of these statements and use them liberally in your speech. It is important, however, to remember that you must match your tone of voice, facial expressions, and body language with the words you use.

Tips to Show Confidence for Assertive Communication

Practice the following stances:
- Stand up straight and make eye contact with your reflection in the mirror. This same technique will help you make eye contact during your interactions with other people.
- Sit in a relaxed manner that exudes confidence
- Practice greeting people when you meet them for the first time. Write down greeting phrases and sentences, and practice them either on your own or with like-minded friends
- Try different clothing to see which suits your personality the best
- Practice courteousness and pleasing conversations

Listening Skills for Assertive Communication

Being assertive requires you to be sensitive to other people's needs, views, and opinions. For this, you should practice listening skills so that you can listen to their perspectives, wants, and desires. Being assertive requires you to sometimes keep aside your views and concerns so that you can focus on those of the other people. Here are some tips to improve your listening skills:

Maintain eye contact with the speaker – Give your full attention to the speaker during the conversation. Avoid working on your computer or looking at your mobile phone or talking on the phone while someone is speaking to you. Maintain reasonable eye contact with the speaker.

Pay attention but remain relaxed – Pay attention to the speaker but ensure you don't come across as tense. Remain calm and relaxed by screening out mental distractions from your mind.

Don't judge – Keep an open mind and don't judge a person based on what he or she says. Assertiveness calls for you to respect the right of everyone, including yourself, to have their own views and opinions. This element helps to improve your listening skills as well. When you keep an open mind and listen to people without judgment, it gives you room to accept their viewpoint wholeheartedly and without malice.

Don't interrupt and impose your solutions – Interrupting people while they are talking sends signals of aggressive behavior. Wrong messages that are sent include:

- What I am saying is more important than what you are trying to say
- I don't have the time or energy for your opinion
- I am more important than you are
- It doesn't matter to me what you think

All of us talk and think at different speeds. If you think and talk faster than your friend, it doesn't give you the right to expect your friend catch up to your speed. On the contrary, assertiveness requires that you reduce your speed to ensure that the other person's right to express his or her views is not violated.

Handling Criticism for Assertive Communication

There are three ways of handling criticism in an assertive manner:

1. If the criticism makes sense or there is truth in it, then agree with it., for example, if your best friend came to you and said, "Why did you have to interfere between my mother and me? You are always poking your nose into my affairs?" If you believe there is some truth in your friend's words, then the right way to respond assertively to this criticism is, "Yes, I do agree that sometimes I get too deeply involved in your affairs. However, I hope you realize the reason for that is you are my friend and I am concerned for your welfare."

2. If the criticism is a result of a mistake, don't hesitate to accept the mistake without rancor. Making a mistake does not make you a bad person. It is perfectly alright to accept your error with humility. For example, if your teacher looked at your homework and said, "What happened to you? You had to do Exercise 13D not 13C!" Your response should be, "Oops. I am so sorry, ma'am. I will resubmit my homework after making corrections."

3. If the criticism is unfounded, tell the person in no uncertain terms that you don't appreciate what is happening. For example, a classmate noticed that your jeans were too short in the morning, to which you have already responded. If he or she continues to make a big issue of it, don't hesitate to respond with something like, "What is your problem exactly? How are my short jeans affecting you in any way? I don't like your repeated reminders."

Here are some classic examples of people who failed and took a lot of criticism in the right way before they achieved success:

Milton Hershey – The man who gave us the delicious milk-chocolate treat was not an immediate hit. He failed multiple times and his products were criticized. He took all feedback given to him, went back to the drawing board, and kept trying until he perfected the delicious milk chocolate that we all love so much today.

Theodore Geisel – Famously called Dr. Seuss, Theodore

Geisel was a highly popular children's author, cartoonist, animator, screenwriter, and a man of many more talents. His works were rejected 27 times by multiple publishing companies as 'pure rubbish.' The man simply refused to give up even in the face of such hurtful criticism. He persisted until he achieved success.

Stephen King – His first work was rejected a whopping 30 times before it became the legendary *Carrie*. He faced criticism after criticism for his writing. He treated every feedback in the right way, corrected his mistakes, and achieved fame in the world of writing. Today, over 350 million copies of his books have been sold the world over.

Final Wrap-Up Tips

- Value yourself as well as the people around you
- Think before you say something; is it fair, just, and respectful?
- Discuss your desires and needs openly
- Remain calm and collected during the interaction
- Keep your eyes and mind open to new perspectives about yourself and the world around you
- Give praise wholeheartedly.
- Take compliments also wholeheartedly and without arrogance
- Take criticism in the right spirit, and work on it if it makes sense. If it does not make sense, simply thank the person for his or her opinion (you give them their right) and choose to ignore (you respect your right too)

And, finally, remember you don't live on an island. Human

beings are social creatures and we live together in communities. We need each other to thrive in this world. Respect this power of humankind, and your ability to build your assertiveness will get a boost.

Chapter 7: Tools to Build Assertiveness

Body language speaks volumes about your level of assertiveness. Your sitting and standing postures, use of gestures, a simple handshake, and the way you present yourself to other people can change your communication style. For example, if your body is slouched, you come across as weak and inhibited.

Why are body language and nonverbal cues so important? Nonverbal communication is one of the primary components of communication amongst human beings. The way you sit in front of somebody communicates something to that person. Similarly, when you see someone standing in front of you, his or her standing posture communicates something to you.

In fact, body language is such a deeply ingrained aspect of our communication that people have learned to make sweeping judgments based on certain body language cues which are universally accepted across cultural and geographical barriers.

Interestingly, our nonverbal cues and body language can

also affect our personality and behavior. For example, in the animal kingdom, the behavior of dominance, aggression, and control was characterized by expansion gestures. Primarily, it was observed that animals 'opened up' or featured expansive gestures like spreading out the arms or spreading out their wings (in the case of animals) or expanding the chest area to reflect dominance over others. This is true of human beings too.

Have you seen images of athletes crossing the finish line? The most common gesture is to spread out and lift their arms in the form of a V. This expansion reflects a sense of power. Contrarily, when we feel powerless, we slouch, make ourselves small by wrapping our arms around us instead of spreading them out. It is as if we don't want to bump into the person standing next to us.

Similarly, when you see two people at different power hierarchies standing next to each other, you will see that they are complementing their power gestures. For example, suppose you are standing next to your teacher because she has called you out for not submitting your assignments on time or have turned in badly done work.

Notice the way you stand; with your arms in front, and your palms joined together in a humbling kind of gesture, and looking up at your teacher. Look at your teacher, and it is very likely that she is standing with her hands on her hips looking down at you.

Now, take a scenario wherein you are in a position. Suppose you are a senior pulling up a junior class student for something; you will notice that you are standing with your hands on your hips and looking down at the junior.

The smaller boy or girl is looking up at you with palms held together in front.

So, in front of someone more powerful than us, we tend to take on a smaller profile, and in the presence of someone more powerful, we tend to take on a larger profile. The dominating body language is referred to as power pose.

Power Poses to Increase Assertiveness

Research studies have proven that confident and assertive people tend to share similar mindsets as well as similar hormonal levels. Interestingly, it was observed that powerful leaders tend to have low levels of cortisol and high levels of testosterone.

Cortisol levels are associated with anxiety and stress. So, reduced levels of cortisol translate to lowered levels of stress which helps in improved anxiety management. The higher the level of testosterone, the higher the confidence level. This was observed for both men and women.

Therefore, if you have lowered cortisol level and high testosterone level, then you tend to feel confident, assertive, and very relaxed. Concurrently, you will be able to control your reactions to stressful and pressure situations. Thus, the correct level of hormones in your body can increase your level of assertiveness.

Moreover, the levels of both these hormones, namely cortisol and testosterone, can change significantly and rapidly based on environmental, physical, and mental cues within and around you. And body language is one of those cues that can alter levels of cortisol and testosterone. Therefore, by controlling your body language, you can control your level of assertiveness and confidence.

Based on the results of various research studies, power poses were designed to help in increasing assertiveness level. The most popular power pose is called the "Wonder Woman" pose, in which you stand erect with your hands on your hips and your head held high. This works for both men and women.

For example, if you have to get on stage to give a speech, and your level of confidence is ebbing due to stage fright, then take a couple of minutes to stand in the 'Wonder Woman' pose before going on stage. Your level of confidence will go up a few notches.

You can also make this power pose your morning routine. Every morning after you get ready to go school, stand in the "Wonder Woman" pose for a couple of minutes. Then, leave for school feeling more refreshed, confident, and assertive than before.

More Assertiveness Tools and Techniques

1. Visualize situations where you will stand up for your rights. For example, if you are the target of bullying, then imagine a situation in which you firmly stand up

for your rights and fend off the bullies successfully. Visualizing self-assertive behaviors helps in the following ways:

- It activates the subconscious mind, resulting in the generation of creative ideas to be more assertive
- It programs your brain to recognize and receive the required resources to increase assertiveness
- It activates the law of attraction by bringing the resources, people, and other elements you will need to be more assertive.
- It increases your internal motivation to improve your assertiveness skills

2. Increase your self-awareness to become more assertive. Assertiveness is all about communication, and you cannot communicate effectively if you don't know yourself well. Therefore, get to know yourself better. Here are some tips:

- Make a list of all the negative elements in your life including those that others see in you.
- Cross out those elements beyond your control. For example, if you have mentioned you are aging, then this element is not under your control. You simply have to accept it, like it, and learn to live with it in the best possible way. Other examples of such negative elements include death, disease, etc.
- Put a tick against those negative elements that you believe you can accept easily
- Circle those problems that you cannot accept but can control. For example, your inability to take criticism is something that you cannot accept but you can learn to overcome.

3. Love yourself. Louise Hay, the motivational author said, "Loving yourself can work many miracles in your life." If you don't love yourself first, no one else will love or respect you. Charity begins at home, and love begins with yourself. Moreover, self-love increases your assertiveness skills considerably. Here are some tips to love yourself:

- Learn ways to enjoy being alone. Starting a hobby is a great idea.

- Travel as much as you can. Seeing the world from a place other than your home can change the way you look at yourself. Moreover, traveling pushes you out of your comfort zone, and when you realize that you can have fun even when you are out of your comfort zone, your self-esteem will take a boost.

- Forgive yourself for mistakes. We all make mistakes. Don't hold old errors against yourself. Learn from the errors, forgive yourself, and move on.

- Start a journal. Writing down your emotions and thoughts will help you understand how you coped with a given situation and help you to find ways to improve upon it.

- Cut yourself some slack. Many of us are very hard on ourselves. We want to do many things and do all of them perfectly and error-free. Such a perfectionist attitude can harm you more than do you good. You will keep finding fault with everything you do, which will result in self-loathing. Therefore, stop being hard on yourself, and let yourself go at times.

- List your accomplishments. Many times, in our busy lives, we forget many of the old achievements that brought laurels to us and our loved ones. Go back to those happy times and make a list of your accomplishments. You can look at this list whenever you are in the dumps.

- Challenge yourself. Sometimes, excessive routine leads to boredom which, in turn, brings on self-loathing. Challenge yourself occasionally and get out of your comfort zone. Success will motivate you. And even if you failed, you can use the learning to get better.

4. Work on your self-esteem. Low self-esteem is one of the primary causes of low levels of assertiveness. Here are some simple tips for building self-esteem:

- Don't compare yourself with anyone else. You are unique. Love and accept yourself the way you are; warts and all.
- Identify your uniqueness and thrive in it. Albert Einstein said, "Each one of us is a genius. However, if you teach a fish to climb a tree, the poor thing will lead its life thinking it is stupid." Therefore, don't be the fish that is being taught to climb the tree. Focus on finding your ocean and become the best swimmer you were born to be.
- Don't miss out on your physical health. Multiple studies have proven the deep connection between exercising and self-esteem. Make sure you get your dose of daily exercise. Or, simply play your favorite sport every day.
- Indulge in a volunteering service. When you see other people, who are worse off than you, and you find an opportunity to help them achieve happiness, even if for a short period of time, you will feel good, and your self-esteem will get an immediate boost.

Use any of these techniques and increase your

assertiveness to garner the multiple benefits it offers to you and those around you.

Chapter 8: Conclusion

Assertiveness is a powerful trait that offers multiple benefits to teenagers on the threshold of a great life. It would be naïve to not spend time and energy on building this important life skill in your adolescent years to leverage these lifelong advantages, including:

Assertive Adolescents Don't Get Bullied

A teenager who stands up and fights for his or her rights is not likely to get bullied. When bullies hear your confident voice saying, "Stop that right now," or "I don't like this," they are quite likely to back off. Additionally, the strength of your assertiveness could increase the resolve of other victims to stand up against bullies.

Assertive Adolescents Don't Indulge in Aggressive Behavior

Verbal and physical aggression does not get anyone anywhere. In fact, such behaviors hurt the aggressor more than the victim. When you build your assertiveness skills, you don't need to show aggression because you will be able to express your opinions in a fair and open manner.

Assertive Adolescents are Great Communicators

As an assertive teenager, you will have learned and mastered the theories of communication and why assertive behavior is the best form of communication. You will have also identified the personal core values that drive you. You know about your current level of assertiveness and what areas need improvement. You have learned the art of altering limiting beliefs that came in the way of success. You have practiced assertive communication skills, and also know other tools and techniques to build assertiveness.

Armed with all these resources (all of which are discussed in this book), you will be very well-equipped to become a great communicator. You know the right thing to do, and you know how to get it done. This oozing confidence will help you to articulately present your case, ensuring that your peers, parents, and teachers know your opinions, feelings, and views.

Assertive Adolescents Have Healthy Relationships

Your excellent communication skills, your ability to state your opinions firmly but gently, your respect for other people's rights, and other important traits related to assertiveness will help you maintain healthy negativity-free relationships with everyone around you. You act responsibly, you handle peer pressure prudently, and are in control of your life. Who will not like to have great relationships with such assertive people?

Assertive Adolescents Have High Self-Esteem

When you learn to speak up for yourself, your level of self-confidence will increase over time which, in turn, builds your self-esteem.

Assertive Adolescents Understand the Power of Emotions

When you are assertive, it means recognize and understand the power of your emotions. You have learned to manage your feelings prudently without them taking control of your life, thereby empowering you to handle all stressful and pressure situations very well.

Now that you have a basic idea of the importance and value of assertiveness in your life, reread the book to reiterate what is being said into your psyche. As you read the book, redo the exercises, quizzes, and journal templates again so that you know exactly what you need to do to build and grow your assertiveness.

If you need more information, helpful tips, and suggestions about general motivation, confidence, self-esteem, and assertiveness, subscribe to our email list. You can also buy books specifically on Self-Esteem for Teens and Confidence for Teens by the same author. We'll finish with this famous quote on assertiveness by Miley Cyrus, the teenage superstar: "If you believe in yourself, then anything is possible." So, believe in yourself and get ahead in life. You are born for a life of joy, happiness, and success.

Part 3: Self Esteem for Teenagers

Six Proven Methods for Building Confidence and Achieving Success in Dating and Relationships

By

Maria van Noord

Chapter 1: What is Self-Esteem?

Self-esteem, many times referred to as self-respect or self-worth, is a personality trait that plays a crucial role in the success of an individual. Another commonly accepted notion of self-esteem is that it is an individual's opinion about himself or herself. The level of your self-esteem depends on many factors and self-beliefs, such as:

- Do you believe you are doing a job worthy of your capabilities and qualifications? Do other people respect you for what you do?
- Do you think you are successful?
- What kind of self-image do you have?
- How do you feel about your weaknesses and strengths?
- Are you constantly comparing yourself with others and finding fault with yourself?
- What do you believe is your standing in your community and social circle?

In psychology, self-esteem is used to describe an individual's overall sense of personal value or self-worth. So, self-esteem can be defined as a measure of how much you like and appreciate yourself for what you are and do.

Self-esteem is a complex phenomenon because it is not a

140

one-dimensional, easy-to-figure-out element of human life. It includes a multitude of beliefs and ideas including physical appearance, level of emotional quotient, behavioral tendencies, and more.

Like all things in the world, the self-esteem trait should also be balanced in an individual for optimal efficacy.

If a person has too little of this important personality characteristic, then he or she can feel disappointed and depressed. Such people will not even get into any venture in the first place because they lack self-belief and self-confidence - both of which are interminably intertwined with self-esteem.

Signs of low self-esteem include a lack of confidence, inability to articulate your needs and desires, focusing excessively on your weaknesses, feelings of anxiety, shame, depression, and fear of failure. Low self-esteem fuels your negative thoughts, weakens your resolve and makes you believe that you are how others perceive you.

On the other hand, people with excessive self-esteem could end up having a narcissistic personality; which is again self-destructive, frequently damages personal and professional relationships irrevocably, and is quite easily one of the most off-putting traits in a person.

Healthy self-esteem is crucial for success, happiness, contentment, and staying motivated to meet and overcome the challenges you encounter in your life. Here are some signs of healthy self-esteem: confidence, the ability to refuse or say no, a positive outlook, the ability to identify and accept strengths and weaknesses, not being unduly impacted by negative experiences, and the ability to articulate your needs and desires.

Is self-esteem nature or nurture? While there is a biological and genetic connection to our behavior and that of our parents and grandparents, genetics and biology do not decide our destiny and cannot really interfere with what we want to become. Moreover, none of us are really born with low self-esteem.

Look at babies from different cultural, racial, and economic backgrounds, and you can see there is hardly any difference in the way they behave. They smile when they are comfortable, fed, and happy. They cry if they are hungry, sleepy, or uncomfortable. No other emotion is really visible in a child.

As babies grow and interact with people around them and get influenced by what they see, hear, and sense, new emotions come to the fore and self-esteem along with its myriad layers of self-confidence, assertiveness, and more also makes an appearance. Low self-esteem is invariably a result of external circumstances, and our interactions with and reactions and responses from other people.

Challenges for Modern-Day Teenagers

Teenage years or the time of adolescence is, perhaps, one of the most sensitive and difficult phases of your life. Multiple emotional and physical changes are taking place in your body and minds, and many of these changes are beyond your control.

As a teenager, you face various challenges including bullying, tremendous academic pressure, body image issues, relationship woes, addictions of different types such as drugs, TV and electronic devices, and, of course, the wrath of the raging hormones. All these factors drive your anxiety and stress to unhealthy levels.

Signs of low self-esteem in teenagers are numerous including poor academic performance, being a victim of or participating in bullying, unprepared and early sexual activity resulting in frequent teen pregnancies, dropping out of school, criminal behavior, alcohol and drug abuse, and disordered eating.

Likely Causes for Low Self-Esteem in Teenagers

So, if we are not born with low self-esteem what can be the likely causes for developing this? Self-esteem at a teenage level comes from various sources including your parents, peers, and teachers. The people you interact with on a daily basis can affect your opinion about yourself.

Additionally, the thoughts that you focus on also plays an important role in either building up or bringing down your self-esteem. Let us look at some of the reasons for low self-esteem among teenagers a bit in detail so that you can identify your own triggers, and find ways to overcome these challenges:

Negligent or uninvolved parents - When your parents or guardians focus on your good traits, you feel good about yourself, and if they focus excessively on your bad qualities showing little or no patience to give you time to get better, then your self-esteem could be hit badly.

Negative peers – Just like parents, if you are surrounded by peers and friends who focus on the bad excessively then your self-esteem will take a beating. Choosing your social group plays an important role in the way your self-esteem takes shape.

Trauma – Sexual, emotional, physical, or a combination of these kinds of abuses takes a big toll on self-esteem, and if left untreated can create bigger psychotic problems.

Body image – How you perceive your body affects your self-esteem. Do you think you are fat, ugly, have horrible freckles, are too short, too dark, etc.? Then you have a problem with self-esteem because body image plays a significant role in the self-esteem of teenagers.

Unrealistic expectations – Some teenagers expect excessive amounts from themselves. They want to do well in academics, in sports, be popular in their social circles, and more. These unrealistic expectations can make you feel that you are not able to meet your desires and goals which, in turn, results in low self-esteem.

Self-Esteem Self-Discovery Quiz
Answer the following questions to identify your self-esteem levels. Then you can work on filling the gaps:
1. Do you think that people find you boring to talk to?
2. Do you believe that you are always messing things up?
3. Do you think that no-one will notice if you are missing

from a party or social gathering?

4. Do you feel that you are constantly letting down people who love and trust you and that you are not good enough for them?

5. Do you think that you can never achieve anything worthwhile?

6. Do you think you are a failure?

7. Do you think that people will respect and love you only if you are great-looking or successful?

8. Do you think you have to be as good as other people to be included in a social group?

9. Do you think you can never be as skilled as you should be?

10. Do you believe you don't deserve to be loved?

The answers to the above questions are not always a perfect 'yes' or a perfect 'no.' Reflect on the questions for a while. Try to recall events in your life that you can relate to the questions. Use the experiences from these past events to answer the questions. You will be able to discern whether you are happy or unhappy qqqq3zxon.

Chapter 2: The Components of Building Self-Esteem

As a teenager undergoing stresses and anxieties, healthy self-esteem will not only help you do well in school and be a stellar performer among your peers and friends but will also be the cornerstone of your adult life. As you step out alone into the big wide world, you will find the courage and strength needed to stave off and overcome challenges thrown at you and emerge strong, happy, and contented with your efforts in particular and your life in general.

Nathaniel Branden, a qualified psychotherapist, was one of the most influential writers on the subject of self-esteem. In his book 'The Six Pillars of Self-Esteem,' Nathaniel Branden has spoken about the six crucial components of self-esteem which include:

1. Living consciously
2. Self-acceptance
3. Self-responsibility
4. Self-assertiveness
5. Purposeful living
6. Personal integrity
7. Let us look at each of these six components in a bit of detail.

The Practice of Living Consciously

As a teenager, you might not yet have been introduced to the concept of conscious living. You get up each morning, get ready, go to school, attend classes, do your assignments, prepare for tests, go out with friends, have relationships, and do everything else that a growing adolescent will do without giving much thought to each of these activities. You live like a robot but breathe like a human being.

Now, living consciously would mean being aware of your feelings, emotions, and sensations as you do each of these activities. So when you wake up each morning, pause for a while, and gather your thoughts. What are you thinking? Are you looking forward to the day? What is it that you are looking forward to? Is it a particular class or meeting up with your partner, or something else?

Be aware of your feelings when you wake up. Similarly, when attending a class, observe your classmates and observe your teacher's voice, his or her words and engage in the class, all the while being aware of how you are behaving and feeling. Be conscious of every activity you indulge in during the day.

Without self-awareness or conscious thought, we are frequently giving in to our emotions instead of thinking calmly and objectively about a given situation. When we make an effort to be self-aware and do everything consciously, we will identify those situations when our emotions are taking over our minds and compelling us to react in a particular way.

147

When you can identify such situations, you can make the necessary corrections and behave and respond in a better way than before. Living consciously is the first step to becoming self-aware which, in turn, helps you improve yourself and work constructively to build your self-esteem.

The Practice of Self-Acceptance

Nathaniel Branden says that 'self-esteem is what we feel and self-acceptance is what we do!' Self-acceptance is accepting yourself the way you are, without a feeling of like or dislike. It is simply, "This is who I am." Let me illustrate with an example. Suppose you are a great football player, and you have won your team many matches. So, you are confident of this skill and you are full of self-esteem on the football field.

Now, shift to the classroom. Your level of academic skill may not be as good as the toppers in the class. Does that mean you should have low self-esteem in class? Not really. The trick is in self-acceptance. Identifying and accepting your strengths and weaknesses without being judgmental is the second most important component of self-esteem.

Accepting your weakness or strength has nothing to do with whether you like it or not. It is simply accepting yourself for what and who you are. Self-acceptance only means to allow yourself to be who you are, without having to seek approval from other people. At this point in time, you are fine with who you are. Acceptance of a weakness does not in any way mean that you are stuck there. In fact, it is the first step to making improvements so that you can overcome that particular weakness.

Interestingly, this self-acceptance includes the acceptance of your resistance to accepting yourself the way you are, if such a situation exists in your life! So, importantly, remember that it is perfectly alright to be who you are at the moment. The future can always be changed for the better. But, right now, don't regret being that person and having a particular personality that combines some strong and some weak traits. Self-acceptance is the reflection of your determination to improve yourself.

The Practice of Self-Responsibility

After self-awareness and self-acceptance are done with, you have to move on to the third important component of self-esteem: self-responsibility. If you continue to see yourself as a victim, it means you are looking for the person or situation victimizing you to change so that you can improve. That is never going to happen because being a victim means you are not in control because the seeming victimizer is holding control of your life. Consequently, your self-esteem is never going to improve.

Taking responsibility for yourself is taking back control of your life. Nobody can take responsibility for our happiness and fulfillment but ourselves. You might get help from people who love and care for you, but your ultimate ability to achieve a satisfying level of self-fulfillment will come only when you take responsibility for everything in your life.

For example, if the top person in your class is not helping

you with a particularly difficult chapter, don't blame him. Simply find another source which can help you. It could be your teacher, the internet, another topper, or someone else in a different class. You have to take responsibility that you need help in that chapter and find ways to learn and master it. Instead if you sit doing nothing except wallowing in self-pity that you are not getting help, this will not raise your self-esteem.

In fact, remember one little thing. If someone is not willing to help you, he or she is truly contributing to your success because now you will be compelled to rely on yourself to do what you thought would be done by someone else. When you are driven to do something you will learn to do it well, and your self-esteem will automatically get a shot in the arm. The person who refuses to help you is facilitating the practice of self-responsibility.

No one can make you happy. If you are waiting for that perfect relationship to make you happy, then you'll wait forever because no perfect person will be coming to save your life. Stop waiting for help; take responsibility for yourself and get to work.

Also, you can be and are responsible only for the things that you can control. For example, suppose you have worked hard, did a test and scored better than your previous time. But the topper has still managed to do better than you. Take responsibility for your work and your efforts which helped you get better grades than you did before. You cannot take responsibility for what the topper did, and feel bad that you could not beat him. That is not in your control.

Take cognizance of the things that you can control and those that you cannot control. Typically, this part of learning about self-responsibility can also be included in the living consciously component of self-esteem. As you live consciously, you will be able to differentiate and accept things that you can and cannot control.

The Practice of Self-Assertiveness

Assertiveness is a term that is referred to a personality trait that is useful at getting you what you want. It is typically associated with getting something extra for yourself and your team. An assertive person is one who holds an advantageous position at a negotiation table over someone whose assertiveness qualities are found wanting.

Self-assertiveness is a little deeper than this, and means you have to learn to acknowledge and honor your needs and desires. Living and expressing your life the way you want to is self-assertiveness.

You start the journey of building esteem by first learning to become self-aware through conscious living, then accepting yourself for who you are and the way you are followed by taking responsibility for your own life's fulfillment and happiness.

Now you come to a stage when you learn to identify and honor your needs and values. Another commonly associated term for self-assertiveness is authenticity, which means being true to yourself. However, being self-assertive, in addition to being honest about your wants, needs, and desires to yourself, also means articulating these elements well so that you reflect your original inner personality to the outside world.

Self-assertiveness means being honest about speaking your mind, even if it means being unpopular with people. You must be ready to face aversion if you are genuinely self-assertive. Self-assertiveness, therefore, translates to living to fulfill your expectations in life and not other people's expectations.

Self-assertiveness is not easy to perfect. As you lead your life with increasing consciousness, you will notice that more often than not it is easier to give in and surrender to people's expectations and do their bidding than it is to assert yourself and face unpopularity and even derision.

A classic example of self-assertiveness as a teenager; you are under a lot of peer pressure to go to a party where drugs and booze are bound to flow. You know that you need to complete that important grade-affecting math assignment that's due in a couple of days. You are sure you need to assert yourself and tell your friends you are going to miss this party. However, fearing ridicule from your friends it is typically easier to give in to their pressure than stand your ground and miss the party so that you can complete the assignment.
Such a situation is familiar to many teenagers, right?

The Practice of Living with Purpose

The most successful people in the world are those who had a clear purpose even as young teenagers. Here are a few classic examples:

- Bill Gates was falling in love with computers as a teenager.
- By the time Warren Buffet was 16, he was earning a lot of money for himself and learning the ways of multiplying his money.
- Oprah Winfrey joined her school's debate team knowing for sure she wanted to talk her way through life, and by the time she was 16 she had landed a job as a broadcaster at WVOL, a local radio station in Nashville, where she was going to school.

When you have set a purpose for your life early on, you will have a deliberate direction. Knowing and visualizing your goal will keep you productive and prevent you from straying from your chosen path. When you advance on your path with little or no intention to waver from it, that act itself can be a huge contributor to your self-esteem.

Choosing a goal should be one that is for yourself alone. Of course, taking advice from family and well-wishers is great. But don't allow your life's purpose to be dictated by others' opinions and dreams. Additionally, setting a goal should be specific, including timelines, a list of activities you will indulge in to achieve your goal, and how you will measure your advancements. When you make your progress measurable, you will be to track results and be aware of whether you are on the right path or if you need to make adjustments.

Having a purpose in life facilitates self-discipline driven by the self-monitoring mechanism, using which we can drive and adjust ourselves continuously. Keeping a goal and moving towards it is a great proof that we can rely on ourselves and our capabilities.

The Practice of Personal Integrity

With the above five points, you have taken care of the majority of the elements needed for improved self-esteem. You are working towards your purpose and goal of life. Now you have to ensure that your actions and behaviors are in line with your values. The more your life is aligned with your own values, the more your self-esteem will rise because you will have the confidence that you are sufficiently well-equipped to manage your life and life goals on your own. You have the ability to face and overcome challenges.

Of course, you will face a lot of situations where the 'unpopularity' tag might follow you around.

For example, take the illustration of having to skip that party to complete your assignment. This would typically be based on your life goal of finishing college with flying colors so that your chances for success in the outside world are high. Your popularity among your peers took a dip. But you stayed on course.

The grades at the end of the term will substantiate your stand and personal integrity, and your self-esteem will definitely go up a few notches. The 'unpopularity' tag may not go away but you will not be bothered with it anymore because you have chosen to align your path to your values and chosen to stay on this path, despite difficulties.

Straying from your path might give you a temporary good

feeling because you feel accepted by your friends. But, more importantly, straying from your chosen path is also a reflection of self-rejection which, in turn, will lead to low self-esteem.

Ask yourself who or what is standing in the way of your personal integrity. It is imperative to identify these major obstacles to improving self-esteem and continuously work on them until you live your life happily and on your own terms.

In addition to the above six components of self-esteem, Nathaniel Branden says that self-esteem has two parts: one part is that of self-efficacy which is the confidence you have in your skills to manage certain situations, and the second part is self-respect which means you believe you are worthy of joy and happiness. He further adds that it is better to be confident in your ability to learn and expand your knowledge rather than in your current level of skills and knowledge.

Self-esteem is not about being perfect. It is the acceptance of who we are in any given situation, including those that remind us of our weaknesses and inabilities. The best way to enhance self-esteem is to be open to continuous learning. The more you learn, the better you get. To be in a state of constant learning, you have to always move out of your comfort zone. Discomfort is the best teacher because it drives our body and mind to find ways to get comfortable, resulting in increased learning.

It is not just facing discomfort when it comes to your self-esteem. You must seek discomfort so that your learning curve is always on the rise. The outcome of seeking discomfort and enhancing learning is high self-esteem.

The best part of building self-esteem is the fact that the power for it lies in your hands alone. You don't need to depend on anyone or anything outside of yourself to love, respect, and have a worthy image of yourself. Take this quiz and see where you stand currently when it comes to self-esteem, then use this to help you identify loopholes and work to fill up the gaps.

Self-Assessment Questions for Living Consciously
These are NLP (Neuro-Linguistic Programming) based self-awareness questions that will help you understand your current status of living consciously:

1) Do you see images in your mind?
a) I do not see images or pictures in my mind or I am only minimally aware of them.
b) Sometimes, I see images in my mind. But I don't know that I can control them.
c) I can see images in my mind vividly, and can work with and control them by altering the size, shape, color, etc.

2) Do you hear your inner sounds clearly?
a) I do not hear inner sounds clearly at all. In fact remembering music, conversation details, etc. are difficult for me.
b) I can hear inner sounds, and remembering music is ok. However, I don't know if I can control them or know how to connect with them.
c) I am very aware of the inner sounds playing in my head, and can control them by adjusting their volume, altering their sound, tone, pitch, location, etc.

3) How deeply do you connect with your feelings?

a) Not much at all. I'm more of a head person.

b) Sometimes I am aware of my emotions. But I don't know how to control them.

c) I am very much in touch with my feelings. I can differentiate between them, label them, convert negative to positive and vice versa, etc.

4) What triggers set off reactions from you?

a) I have no idea what sets me off; when I feel bad I simply react.

b) I do have triggers, and if I think deeply enough I could come up with a couple of them. But I don't think proactively about these triggers, and I don't know what to do with them.

c) I know exactly which stimulus sparks me off. I am aware when I'm not reacting in a nice way. I can often identify the trigger that makes me do so.

5) Do you know your limitations? Are you aware of the things you are good at and those that are you are not good at?

6) Do you know your personal beliefs and values? Do you know your capabilities?

7) Do you know what you value the most in your life?

8) What are your inner conflicts?

9) What kind of parental impact have you had on your life? How do your interactions with them affect you?

10) What about your peers and partners? How do they impact your life?

Self-Assessment Questions for Self-Acceptance
1) Do you keep comparing your capabilities with those of other people to feel worthy?
2) Do you set goals based on what others want?
3) Do you frequently attempt to categorize yourself as good, bad, average, etc.?
4) Do you feel pained, angry, hurt or resentful if you or your work is criticized?
5) Do you focus excessively on the weaknesses which make you dislike your personality?

Self-Assessment Questions for Self-Responsibility
1) Do you believe that your actions and behaviors are reflective of how you want to lead your life?
2) Do you think that your reactions are your responsibility, irrespective of what caused the reactions?
3) Do you take responsibility for your physical health and ensure you take your dose of exercise, good nutrition, and restful sleep?
4) Do you believe that you are responsible for your happiness?
5) Do you think your values and principles of life should be your choice and not those of your parents, peers, friends, etc.?
6) Do you make the effort to seek help when you need it?

Self-Assessment Questions for Self-Assertiveness
1) Do you take pains to do what you believe in, even if it means being unpopular with people who care about you and love you?
2) Do you make efforts to live your life based on your

values and principles?

3) Do you believe that even if you need to be present in a place that you don't like, how you choose to spend quality time there is up to you?

Self-Assessment Questions for Purposeful Living

1) Where do you see yourself when you are twenty years old; in college or somewhere else?

2) Have you set clear, specific, timebound, and measurable goals for yourself?

3) Do you keep track of your progress?

4) What are the triggers that drive you away from your goals? What helps you stay on course?

Self-Assessment Questions for Personal Integrity

1) How often do you lie to your parents, teachers, and peers?

2) Do you think you will accept a mistake you make if you think there is an easy way to get away with it?

3) Do you believe you lead a life that is aligned with your goals and purposes?

Chapter 3: Habits and How to Use Them for the Good

Habits are behaviors or rituals that we perform automatically without thinking. Human beings are creatures of habit, and we continue to activate new habits every day. Typically, habits can be divided into three categories:

1. Habits we don't notice – such as brushing our teeth, tying our shoelaces, etc.
2. Good habits – like going for your morning run every day, sleeping and waking up on time each day.
3. Bad habits – like smoking, procrastinating, addictions to video games, etc.

All of us want to cultivate good habits and get rid of bad habits. Habits are so complex that understanding and changing them by diagnosing each of them separately can be quite a challenge. Moreover, each bad habit is unique and calls for a different technique in order to be broken. For example, breaking the bad habit of smoking requires a different tactic from breaking the bad habit of excessive eating.

Charles Duhigg, in his book 'The Power of Habit,' discussed the habit loop through which he attempts to

160

show readers that by understanding how habits work, it is possible to change any bad, unproductive habit into a useful and productive one. He speaks of a simple neurological loop that can cover any habit you have, and then shows you how to use effective methods to alter or eliminate the habit suitably.

The neurological loop of any habit consists of:
- The Cue
- The Routine
- The Reward

If you can identify the component loops of your bad habits, you can find ways to replace bad habits with good ones.

The Cue

A cue is typically a trigger that puts your brain into an automatic mode and drives it to follow a habit without thinking. Here are some types of cues that trigger a habit:

Time – This is the most common trigger of habits. Regular morning habits are a classic example. You wake up, walk into the bathroom, brush your teeth, take a shower, get dressed, have breakfast or a cup of coffee, and get to class or lab or any other college-related activity.

Identify the cue for the bad habit. Now, look at your bad habit and pay attention to see if there is a specific time that triggers it. For example, do you walk to your college cafeteria for a plate of fries at around 11 in the morning or 3 in the afternoon? If yes, then take stock of your feelings during those times. Is it hunger or boredom or loneliness that makes you do that?

Use this cue to replace the bad habit with a good one. So, at around the time when the bad habit kicks off, place reminders to focus on something productive. For example, keep your books close to you so that you can use that time cue to start reading or writing your assignment. If it is hunger, then make sure you have some healthy snack in your bag to dig into.

Location – Another powerful cue to set off habits is your location. For example, how many times have you walked into the kitchen to reach into a jar of cookies and eaten a couple of them without thinking? Now to change the habit to something good, keep away cookies so that you can't reach or see them and so will not get a chance to eat them. Additionally you can replace the cookie jar with a bowl of fruit so that you change your habit of eating healthy food.

Preceding events – A great example of this is when your phone rings. After you answer your call, invariably your brain is tuned to check out your social media notifications. Now, you can use such preceding event illustrations to set up good habits.

For instance, you can create a habit of meditating for a couple of minutes while you are getting your morning coffee or breakfast. Or you could make a note of two things that happened during the day that you are grateful for when you sit down for your evening meal, or just before retiring to bed.

Emotional status – Have you reached for the ice-cream whenever you felt depressed? Or have you gone on a shopping spree when you are angry or upset? The emotional states of anger or sadness are perfect cues to set off bad habits.

Identifying an emotional state to start off a good habit is a much bigger challenge than using cues like time, location, etc. Emotions can unwittingly overpower us. So it might make sense, at least initially, to only prevent yourself from behaving rashly instead of trying to replace your bad habit.

Recognizing the emotional status cues and simply paying attention mindfully to the emotion can help to prevent you from moving into the routine part of the habit. You could perform basic breathing exercises during times of emotional stress, and see how much difference that makes.

Other people – The people around you have a big impact on the habits that you inculcate. Studies have proven that if you are surrounded by obese friends, the chances of you becoming obese are higher than if you are surrounded by fit and healthy people.

So, the most effective way to inculcate and build good habits is to surround yourself by friends who have good habits. If you need to go to the gym each morning, make friends with someone who never misses his or her gym time. If you wish to eat healthily, make friends with people who count calories during their meals. If you wish to improve in your academics, make friends with the toppers and the studious people in your class.

If you want to break the habit of smoking, stay away from friends who smoke. If you want to quit excessive partying, stay away from friends who host and attend too many parties.

The Routine

The routine is the physical, emotional or mental action that you take after your brain receives the cue. In the examples stated above, the routine was in the form of:

- Walking into the college cafeteria at 11 in the morning and/or 3 in the afternoon
- Putting your hand into the jar of cookies when you walk into the kitchen
- Looking at social media notifications when you receive a call
- Binge-eating or going out shopping when depressed
  You also looked at how you can use the cues of time, location, preceding events, and emotional status to convert your bad-habit routines into good-habit routines such as:
- Keeping books with you so that you can study instead of walking to the cafeteria
- Replacing the jar of cookies with a bowl of fruit
- Using preceding events to remind you to meditate or write thank-you notes
- Meditating during bouts of high emotion instead of indulging in retail therapy or binge-eating

The Reward

The reward is that ultimate prize or end result of the habit which helps your brain to determine whether this particular loop is worth the effort of keeping in and recalling from memory. The reward is typically stored as a craving in your brain which drives the habit loop. In the above examples, rewards are typically the joy of eating that plate of fries or cookies or reading up interesting but useless gossip on social media or the act of retail therapy.

To change your habits, you can experiment with rewards instead of depending only on what the bad habits promise you. For example instead of walking to the college cafeteria, why don't you walk to the college library? If meeting with friends is the reward for the walk to the cafeteria, why don't you fix a different place for that? Convert the joy of eating a cookie into the joy of drinking a glass of fresh juice.

The way to build healthy habits and get rid of bad habits is to recognize the habit loop and get your brain to alter the cues, routines, and rewards suitably.

Self-Assessment of Bad Habits
Look at the following common bad habits among teenagers, and ask yourself if you are a victim of any of them:
- Biting fingernails
- Chewing gum
- Complaining
- Procrastinating
- Drinking excessively
- Smoking cigarettes or pot
- Excessive junk food
- Lack of exercising
- Spending too much time on the internet

- Coming late
- Playing online games or gambling
- Spending too much money
- Using bad words
- Gossiping
- Not showing gratitude
- Shopping when you're hungry
- Not saving money
- Dressing shabbily
- Binge-watching
- Breaking relationships without letting your partner know; ghosting relationships
- Leaving your dishes in the sink thinking your parents will handle them
- Telling white lies; a classic example of saying you turned in your assignment without actually having done so
- Not planning your study

Some of these habits might appear innocuous. But the unfortunate thing about bad habits picked up during your teenage years is that they invariably last your entire lifetime. And, fortunately, good habits picked up during your teenage years also last your entire lifetime. Therefore it makes a lot of sense to spend time and energy to break bad habits and build good ones. Moreover, bad habits during teenage years will not have typically reached the irreversible stage making it relatively easy to get rid of them.

Step-by-Step Guide to Starting Good Habits
Step 1 - Identify the habit you want to start. Define the

cue that will trigger the start of your routine. At what time is the cue most likely to be triggered (time)? Where will you be when the cue is triggered (location)? What will be the preceding event? What will be your emotional status?

Step 2 - Define the rewards when the routine is done. Do you crave this reward? How do you feel when you get the reward?

Step 3 - Define the routine.

Step 4 – Put all these elements together and write the new habit down. Make sticky notes of the new habits and put them up at unmissable places so that your memory is triggered at the right times and in the right locations.

Here is a simple example: When I see (preceding event) my toothbrush at night, I will brush (routine) my teeth for that lovely, clean, and fresh feeling in my mouth (reward).

Step-by-Step Guide to Breaking Bad Habits

Step 1 – Identify the bad habit you want to break. What is the cue for it? What time? Where? Who are the people around you? What are the preceding events? What is your emotional status?

Step 2 – Define the reward or the craving the bad habit is satisfying. Experiment with other rewards that give similar satisfaction. You have to keep experimenting with your rewards until you find the ones that make the craving of the bad habit go away.

Step 3 – Now, define the routine and put the entire thing together. Make sticky notes and place reminders all over to ensure you don't fall for the wrong cues and experiment with new rewards.

Chapter 4: Practical Examples

This chapter is dedicated to giving you practical examples of how you can build self-esteem by building on the six components discussed in Chapter 2.

The Practice of Living Consciously

NLP techniques

NLP or Neuro Linguistic Programming helps you 'upgrade your mind.' NLP techniques help with improving your intelligence, memory, mindset, and communication skills by aligning your conscious mind with your unconscious mind. NLP stands for:

- Neuro – pertains to the brain's communication tools; the nerves and the neurons
- Linguistic – pertains to the language of the mind
- Programming – refers to setting something to work in a particular way.

Here are some NLP techniques to help you live your life with improved consciousness:

Pay attention to your thoughts – Our unconscious

minds are affected by what we think about the most. For example, if your thoughts are that you are not going to pass the upcoming school test then your conscious mind and your body are going to resist your attempts to prepare for the test.

Instead, if your thoughts are 'I am going to work hard to pass the school test with flying colors,' then your body and your conscious mind will be aligned with these positive thoughts and you will find it easy to focus on studying hard which, in turn, will definitely help you clear your test well.

Prayers – Prayers are nothing but wishes or hopes that some things will happen the way you want them to. Prayers give you a sense of faith that your wish or hope will come true.

For example, if you repeatedly pray that you get selected for your school's basketball team then your conscious mind adopts it and passes it on to the subconscious mind, and drives your entire bring to believing and accepting the importance of this prayer. Moreover this prayer gives you faith that your expectations will come true, and faith will drive you to work hard to achieve your dreams.

Affirmations

Use affirmations to live consciously. Create positive feelings by using affirmations. Here are some affirmations you can use:

- I deserve to be loved
- I have the power to bring about positive changes in my life
- I am strong enough to make my own decisions

- I have the power to be happy irrespective of external circumstances

Visualization

Visualization helps to direct your mind and body towards the path of your goal without being negatively impacted by the outside world. A classic example of a highly successful person who used their visualization to high levels of success is Nikola Tesla, a man who gave us the AC induction motor, wireless communication, and over 700 patented inventions, many of which are still in use today. Apparently he would build the device in his imagination first, and only then make it a tangible product.

Even though you may think you are not anywhere near Tesla's superhuman levels, his life is an example of the power of visualization that each of us is endowed with. Use it effectively to live consciously. Visualize victories and happy days. Work towards crystallizing those mind visuals.

Meditation

Meditate regularly to connect with your thoughts and emotions. This will help you become more conscious of these elements in your life, and you will be able to discern between good and bad thoughts. For example, start your morning with a 10-minute meditation during which time you can acutely visualize how you want your day to unfold. Make sure you focus on the positives so that you start your day on a positive note which empowers your body and mind to be prepared to take on the challenges of the day.

Maintaining a Diary

Maintaining a diary which you update regularly helps you

in many ways:

First, it makes you more aware of what has happened during the day. For example, suppose a test score was announced in school and your scores were really good. However you did not have time to respond emotionally because the teacher for the next subject walked into class, and you got sucked into the day's activities.

When you sit down to update your diary at the end of the day, you will get the required time to truly appreciate your hard work which paid off by getting you great scores. You become more acutely aware of the happiness of having worked hard for which you got suitably rewarded, thereby improving your connections with your emotions and feelings.

Second, it gives you reasons to feel gratitude. As you pass through your day in a rush, you will not find enough time to think deeply about the many good things that happened to you during the day. When you sit down to make entries in your diary at the end of each day, you will get sufficient time to be grateful for all the good things of the day.

Third, you will find the power to look at the negative things of the day without the attached emotion, which will help you learn important lessons for the future.

The Practice of Self-Acceptance

NLP Techniques
Anchoring for self-acceptance – Anchoring is an NLP technique that allows you to anchor feelings of positivity through the use of a physical sensation.

For example, remember that feeling of happiness you had when you led your school team to victory in the interschool basketball match. Recall the ecstatic feelings associated with that event, and simultaneously rub your index finger and thumb together or touch your right ear or perform any other convenient action. Keep repeating the chosen action each time you recall those great times. This is the anchoring process.

During moments of self-doubt, perform the physical action connected to those happy thoughts. This will help you to overcome self-doubts and accept yourself as you are.

Affirmations

If you don't love and accept yourself first, the chances of others accepting and loving you are low. Self-love and self-acceptance are primary elements of self-esteem. Use affirmations for self-acceptance:

- I am worthy of love, joy, and happiness
- I approve of myself
- I am complete by myself and do not need anything more to complete me
- My life is a gift to me. I will use it with exuberance and confidence
- I will surround myself only with positivity

Visualization

Visualizations can help in building self-acceptance and self-love. Always visualize yourself as being happy and joyful. Imagining yourself as a happy-go-lucky and fun-loving person will make your brain think it to be true, and will create physical impulses and reactions that are aligned with this happy mood.

For example, it is common for a smile to come on your face when you visualize something pleasant. Haven't you come across a situation where a friend has asked you why you are smiling? And only then it has struck you that you have a smile on your face. That is the power of visualization. You visualize something nice, and it gets reflected in your body. Similarly, when you visualize something bad either tears well up or a frown automatically forms on your face.

Self-love through visualization will, therefore, be reflected in your body language. When you love yourself and accept your strengths and weaknesses with humility, your level of confidence takes a boost and it will be reflected in the spring of your step or that confident smile.

Meditation
Use self-acceptance affirmations mentioned below (or create your own) to sit still and meditate whenever you doubt yourself or are going through a difficult patch.

- I trust myself to do my best
- I am unique and original and that is a blessing
- I believe in myself
- I can be loved only when I love myself
- I can love others unconditionally only when I love myself unconditionally
- My opinions are worthwhile and valuable
- My approval is good enough for me

Maintaining a Diary
Write down answers to the following self-acceptance questions. Crystallizing your thoughts into words will help

you improve your level of self-acceptance and self-love.

- What are the things that I know and believe I deserve? Why?
- What is the meaning of trust to me? How can I trust myself more?
- Can you recall a time when you didn't get what you wanted and, later on, you realized it was for the better? Write that event down.

The Practice of Self-Responsibility

NLP Techniques
Swish technique for altering negative thoughts –
The Swish NLP technique is designed to teach your brain to think differently and innovatively to triggers of negativity. By practicing the Swish pattern, you are teaching your brain to use the same old cue but react or respond differently.

Let us take the example of a typical scenario in a teenager's life. You have taken the SAT test, and your scores have turned out average. Now, you've decided to take responsibility for it and you are determined to repeat the test for better scores.

Now, you have prepared for the second round of the SAT. However, you are ridden with self-doubts and fears that are eating into your self-confidence. Take the help of the Swish technique so that you can take responsibility for yourself and redo the test with confidence, and free yourself from needless negative thoughts and fears. The Swish NLP uses four components including:

The unwanted trigger or thought – This is the

negative thought. So, in your case the negative thought is the image of you walking in to do the test and finding all the questions difficult to answer.

The unwanted feeling – This is the feeling that the bad feelings evoke. So, whenever you imagine the SAT test that is difficult to solve your stomach churns, your palms get all sweaty, and you are filled with panic.

Replacement thought – You have done a lot of preparation and have also undergone multiple mock tests in which your scores were really great. So, you pick a memory of one such successful test and replace your unwanted trigger or thought with this happy memory. Keep repeating the Swish test until your mind is rewired to eliminate anxieties and fears.

It is important to remember that the Swish technique works only when the fears are unfounded and have no tangible basis. You know you have prepared hard for the second round of the test, and you are ready to take it. However, needless and baseless self-doubts are preventing you from taking the plunge.

So you use the Swish NLP technique to rid yourself of these baseless doubts, take responsibility for your hard work and outcomes, and go with confidence to do the retest.

Affirmations
Building self-esteem is in your hands. Take responsibility for yourself. Use these affirmations for personal responsibility to help you:
- I am taking 100% responsibility for what happened,

for what is happening, and for what will happen to my life.

- I am responsible for the way my life turns out
- I am certainly not responsible for how others choose to perceive me
- I am responsible for all actions, thoughts, feelings, and words that I experience and use
- I will honor my commitment to becoming self-responsible, even when I don't like the outcomes

Visualization

Visualization is a powerful tool to use to imagine your future life, and then work to make it a reality. Here is a little exercise you can follow to visualize your future life and take responsibility for achieving it:

- First, sit in a calm and relaxed manner.
- Next, close your eyes and imagine what you see yourself as when you step out of your adolescence.
- What do you see in your mind? The gates of a college? The scene of a graduation day when you are walking up to the stage to receive a prize even as you hear thunderous applause for you in the background?
- Don't entertain any doubts at this stage. Fill in all the details of the imagery; the colors, the smells, the sounds, the people who you want to be with you in the future, and every other important detail. Engrave this image into your mind.
- Now, open your eyes and revel in the joy of achieving your dreams in your mind.
- Take responsibility for this visualization, and begin working to make it a reality.

Meditation

Look at the following example: You are doing a stretching asana in a yoga class. Now, your teacher comes close and presses you to stretch a little harder. You are distracted at that moment. However, following his or her instructions you stretch a little more and pull a muscle. Now, whose fault is it?

Yes, you could blame the teacher for being inexperienced and giving you instructions without knowing your body well. However, if you blame your teacher you become powerless to do anything productive in the future because you have passed on the power to your teacher.

Instead, if you took responsibility for what happened and included factors such as;

- Your own distraction
- Your thoughtless action to follow the teacher's instructions
- Acting impulsively
- Ignoring the first couple of minutes of discomfort you got when you stretched more than you should have done

Meditate on the entire episode, and take responsibility for those things that you could've done right to prevent the muscle tear. This way you empower yourself to take control of your life, and not let someone else sit in the driver's seat.

Maintaining a Diary

Make entries in your diary for all the elements of the day

that you disliked. Against each of those elements, make a note of at least two things you could have done or not done which could have altered the outcome favorably for you. Make this a practice, and with each passing day, you will notice your ability to take responsibility for your life improving significantly.

The Practice of Self-Assertiveness

NLP Techniques
One of the most important NLP lessons for self-assertiveness is to learn to say no to people. Do you have friends in your class or neighborhood who take you for granted? Can you recall how many times you have agreed to do the class bully's homework simply to remain in his or her good books, despite knowing you should have said no?

What about wanting to be picked for the school basketball, football, or cheerleading team? In order to be chosen, have you done favors to people who hold powerful positions? All these are classic examples of lack of self-assertiveness during teenage life. It is important to be conscious of these elements and learn the art of saying no when you are being taken for granted or simply to win a favor.

Instead, build your skills and confidence so that you can assert yourself when the situation calls for it. NLP training involves deconstructing and formulating scenarios, assertive responses, and processes that can be used in a real-life situation. Practice assertive responses and reactions when alone and use them confidently when the need arises. The more you practice these scenarios and enactments, the easier it will be for you to use them in real-life situations.

Affirmations

Repeating these affirmations helps in developing a natural sense of assertiveness to express yourself and your thoughts honestly. These affirmations help you to stand up for your beliefs and values, take control when needed, and speak your mind openly and freely.

- I speak my mind without fear
- I am an assertive person
- I do not hesitate to tell others how I feel
- I am confident when talking to people
- I stand firm when needed
- I stand up for my values and principles
- I confidently control a situation if required
- I do not hesitate to express myself honestly
- Assertiveness is a natural trait in me
- I set clear boundaries when required
- Others respect me because I am self-assertive

Visualization

Suppose you had to give a speech in front of the class. It is on a topic that you are really good at, and there is no reason for panic. Yet your lack of self-assertive skills drives you into a panic mode. What do you do? First, ensure you are thoroughly prepared with your speech. Practice the speech multiple times to make sure there are no errors.

Now, sit in a relaxed manner in a chair and close your eyes. Transport yourself in your mind to your class. Imagine all your classmates sitting in their respective places waiting for you to walk up and give your speech.

Now, visualize yourself walking up confidently with your head held high. Imagine yourself standing on the dais, getting ready to give your speech. Imagine smiling confidently.

Repeat the speech in your mind without a mistake. Visualize the confident throw of your voice as you present your ideas. When you finish the speech, visualize getting a great round of applause from your classmates as well as from your teacher. Open your eyes, and feel the confidence of the visualization you just had course through your entire body.

Meditation
Some people mistakenly believe that practicing meditation takes the 'edge off' of self-assertiveness, as you are supported by a mellowed-down attitude brought on by meditation. Nothing can be farther from the truth. Meditation does not make anyone less assertive. On the contrary, it empowers you to handle all situations with lowered levels of stress thereby helping you achieve what you want easily.

Moreover, meditation helps you discern between assertiveness and aggression. It helps you become self-aware thereby giving you the power to articulate your thoughts correctly and in line with your values and principles. Meditate for 15 minutes before you leave for class each day. You can use one of the affirmations like a mantra during your meditation.

Maintaining a Diary
Write down the problems that you faced each day. Next to

each of these problems, write down your affirmations. Write down your visualizations for a more successful outcome than you had on that day.

For example, suppose your worst problem at school one day was to be bullied mercilessly. You felt so miserable at being bullied that the tears of self-pity came naturally, which only increased the bullying. The day finally finished.

Now, write down the three most suitable affirmations for the bullying problem you faced today. Examples could be:
- Bullies cannot undermine my power. Their actions only reflect their own lack of confidence.
- Crying while being mercilessly bullied was not a sign of weakness. It was only a natural response to mental pain. There is nothing to be ashamed about.
- I am proud that I did not hit back or behave aggressively with them.

Now, visualize a similar scenario and imagine yourself coming through the unpleasant episode by standing up for yourself, and telling the bullies sternly and firmly to back off. Reading your thoughts will help you build your self-assertiveness.

The Practice of Living with Purpose

NLP Techniques
A powerful NLP tool for living a purposeful life is to set SMART goals. SMART stands for:

S – Specific goals that are clearly stated; for example, 'I will lose 5 pounds by the end of this quarter' is a specific goal, rather than 'I will lose weight.'

M – Measurable goals mean you can determine easily if you have achieved your goals. So, in the above example 5 pounds can be easily measured whereas the second example does not have any measurable aspect to it, and therefore does not constitute a SMART goal.

A – Achievable goals are those that are possible to be achieved. For example, 'I will study to get a GPA score of 4 or above in order to get into a good college' is an achievable goal, especially if your score until now has been hovering around 3. However, 'I will become the next President of the United States' is not achievable, at least not at this stage in your life.

R – Realistic goals means the goals should be achievable after taking into consideration your current circumstances. For example, if your current GPA is hovering between 1.5 and 2, then setting a goal of 4 within the same semester looks unrealistic. You will have to set goals that increase your GPA scores in stages; first try to achieve a 2.5, then a 3, then a 3.5, and finally to 4 and above.

T – Time-bound means your goals must have an expiry date. For example, 'I will achieve a GPA score of 4' is not timebound whereas 'I will achieve a GPA score of 4 by the 3rd semester of college' is timebound

Affirmations

Here are some examples of affirmations for living with a purpose:

- I am connected with my destiny
- I am aligned with the higher purpose of my life
- I can hear my inner voice telling me where to go

- I live a life of passion and purpose
- I dream and then I work to make my dreams a reality
- I create my own life

Visualization

The following visualizations of your life purpose are highly suited for any adolescent. Feel free to choose one of them or dig deeper into your mind to identify and visualize your own destiny.

- Imagine your graduation day on which your family and friends are proudly watching you walk up to the stage to receive the best student award
- Visualize yourself participating in a national or international meet of your favorite game, and winning the gold medal
- Imagine yourself with a hefty bank balance, with a beautiful home, and a loving family
- Imagine yourself traveling the world and becoming a famous travel-blogger
- Visualize yourself driving a snazzy car of your choice
  Powerful visualizations enhance your willpower and resolve to help you achieve your life purpose.

Meditation

One of the biggest challenges of living with purpose is that the set purpose is forgotten or lost in the din and noise of everyday living. Your daily school grinds, your social circle times, your tests, assignments, partying, and more - such daily activities take up so much of your time and energy that it is very easy to forget what your purpose of life is.

It is, therefore, imperative that you keep reminding yourself of your life goals. Before retiring to bed or as soon as you wake up in the morning, sit for a couple of minutes in silence and solitude and meditate on your life goal. For example, when the alarm rings to wake you up in the morning don't get off the bed immediately. Sit on it, close your eyes, and repeat to yourself your life goal - whatever it may be:

- I promise I will get into a good college to do my computer science engineering
- Five years from now, I see myself working in one of the best law firms as an intern
- Two years from now, I see myself winning a medal at the national level athletics meet

Maintaining a Diary

The SMART goals are best recorded in your diary along with space to update successful and failed milestones. It is important to keep track of your 'life purpose' diary and ensure all entries are made honestly and objectively. Maintaining a diary helps you reflect on your successes and failures.

Moreover, maintaining a diary helps you remain grounded right through your life. How is this possible? Every time you feel discouraged and depressed, take a peek into your diary and read your success stories and get back that feeling of motivation. Every time you feel overconfident and arrogant about your achievements, read your stories of failure to remind yourself that failure is part and parcel of life. You will learn to be grateful for your successes as well as for the lessons from your failures.

The Practice of Personal Integrity

NLP Techniques

Personal integrity is nothing but walking the talk and talking the walk. You do as you say, and you say only what you do. Therefore, practicing a life of personal integrity calls for a deep level of self-awareness because only when you are aware of your values and principles can you live your life aligned with them.

Here are some NLP-based suggestions to practice personal integrity:

- Find the courage to say NO so that you make only those promises that you can keep.
- Learn to be more self-disciplined so that you spend more time doing useful (and promised) things than wasting time in lazing around, attending far more social events than you should, etc.
- Break large jobs into smaller tasks so that it is easy to monitor them and ensure the final promised task is completed on time.

Affirmations

Use the following affirmations to align your heart, mind, and body with your core values and beliefs:

- Everything I say or do is a sincere promise
- I value honesty and integrity above all else
- I practice what I preach
- I do not hesitate to admit my mistakes
- I always do what I believe is right even in the face of dissension and unpopularity
- I promise only when I can keep it

Visualization

Always imagine keeping promises and seeing the happy faces of the people to whom you have kept your promise. For example, suppose you have promised your friend that you will go to her house to help her complete her science project. Now, suddenly, you have received a party invitation from another set of friends. You can go because you have nothing pending to be done. However, you have given your promise to your friend. The choice you make now reflects your personal integrity. Think and then choose.

Meditation

The more we know and appreciate ourselves, the more we get rooted in personal integrity. As you meditate each day and get in touch with the deep parts of your mind, you understand why you are the way you are. This knowledge will help you stay grounded to your core values which, in turn, help you lead an honest and straightforward life with little or no guile.

Moreover, meditation clears your mind of useless thoughts that only confuse and addle you. A clear and calm mind is the cornerstone of personal integrity. You know where you stand and you know what you need to do to remain there.

Maintaining a Diary

Despite our best efforts, there are times when we end up breaking promises. In the above example wherein you had to choose between going to a fun party and helping your friend, it is possible that you chose to break your promise because the lure of the party was too good to resist.

Remember to make a note of such instances in your diary. Don't forget to add the look of pain that came over your friend's face when you made up a lame excuse the next day, or when she found out that you chose the party over your promise.

The next time such a situation comes up again do go back to read what you have written, and hopefully, that will help you improve your personal integrity. The more you face up to your mistakes, the closer you get to becoming an honest and upright person.

Chapter 5: Workbook

This questionnaire or workbook is based on the format of the six components as explained in Chapter 4. You need to invest your time and effort to complete the workbook to be able to slowly but surely build the six components of self-esteem in your life. The workbook is general in nature and is flexible enough to fit into any teenager's life.

Complete the quizzes given in Chapter 2 under the six components of self-esteem. Based on the result, arrange the components in increasing order of importance starting from the one that needs your immediate attention (because you rate yourself the lowest in that) and ending with the one that needs your least attention (because you rate yourself highly on that).

Complete the workbooks in the same order as your customized ranking list. For example, if your biggest concern is to find a purpose in life then do the workbook for that first. If your least concern is to live life with personal integrity, then keep the workbook concerned with that component last.

Workbook for the Practice of Living Consciously

NLP techniques – Paying Attention to Your Thoughts
Before going to bed, write down the three most important thoughts that took hold of your mind today:

1)

_____

_____

_____

_____

_____

_____

_____

2)

_____

_____

_____

_____

_____

_____

3)

_____

_____

_____

_____

_____

_____

_____

NLP Techniques – Prayers

On every Sunday night, write down the three most important prayers that you want answered in the coming week:

1)

_____

_____

_____

_____

_____

_____

_____

2)

_____

_____

_____

_____

_____

_____

3)

_____

_____

_____

_____

_____

_____

Affirmations – Write down the three most important affirmations that are aligned with your efforts to live life more consciously than before:

1)

_____

_____

_____

2)_____

_____

_____

3)_____

_____

_____

Visualization – Visualize one goal in your life, and write it down in great detail including:

The scene

_____

_____

_____

The people in it

_____

—
Smells

_____

_____

_____

Sounds

_____

_____

_____

Your feelings

_____

_____

Meditation – After your meditation session, write down the two most important things that occupied your mind despite your best efforts in trying to keep your focus on meditating:

1)

_____

_____

_____

_____

_____

_____

_____

2)

_____

_____

_____

_____

_____

Maintaining a Diary – At the end of each week, read through your diary and identify one element that recurred at least twice for which you had to show gratitude. If there are more, do make a note of them too;

1)

_____

_____

_____

_____

_____

_____

Workbook for the Practice of Self-Acceptance

NLP Anchoring Technique - Take two of the happiest memories of your life until now, and create anchoring techniques for them so that you have them ready to use whenever needed.

1)

_____

_____

_____

_____

_____

_____

_____

2)

_____

_____

_____

_____

_____

_____

_____

Affirmations – Write down three affirmations for self-acceptance. Think and make your own. Don't copy from what is given in this book:

1)

_____

_____

_____

2)_____

_____

_____

3)_____

_____

_____

Visualization – Write down a detailed description of your happy self. What are the things that make you happy and loved?

_____

_____

_____

_____

_____

_____

_____

Meditation – Focus and meditate on any of the following affirmations for self-acceptance or create and use your own:

I love myself the way I am

I accept my strengths with joy and my weaknesses with humility

Workbook for the Practice of Self-Responsibility

The NLP Swish Technique – Write down three unwanted triggers and the corresponding replacement triggers for each of them:

Unwanted   trigger   1)

Replacement	trigger	1)
Unwanted	trigger	2)
Replacement	trigger	2)
Unwanted	trigger	3)
Replacement	trigger	3)

—

Affirmation – Which of the following self-responsibility affirmations suit you best?
- I take full responsibility for my life.
- I am responsible for whatever happens in my life.
- I honor all commitments in my life, unmindful of deterring obstacles.

Visualization – Write down your most important goal in life, and visualize the day you will achieve it. Write down detailed descriptions of your imagination.

_____
_____
_____
_____

_____

_____

_____

Meditation – Take an example of an event in your life that resulted in pain for you. Think objectively and write down all the contributing factors of the pain. Categorize the factors under two headings:

Under your control

_____

_____

_____

_____

_____

_____

_____

Not under your control

_____

_____

_____

_____

_____

_____

You can use your diary to hunt for such painful situations.

Workbook for the Practice of Self-Assertiveness

NLP Techniques – Look at the following examples and answer honestly:

If you had to choose between staying back to complete your assignment and going for a great party, which would you choose and why?

If you had to choose between a friend who is boring but a topper in class and a friend who is great fun to be with but can lead you astray, who will you choose as your best friend?

Practice answers to these questions so that when a real-life situation comes, your mind is ready to make the appropriate choice backed by sound reasoning.

Affirmations – Complete the following affirmations for self-assertiveness in your own words:
1) I am

_____

2) I am not deterred by

_____

3) I stand up for

_____

Visualization – Think of a situation in your life that keeps repeating in which you find it extremely difficult to say no. Now, visualize the same event in your mind and imagine saying no. Write down the details of your imagination; your words, gestures, body language, tone of voice, etc.

_____
_____
_____
_____

_____
_____
_____
_____

Workbook for the Practice of Living with Purpose

NLP Techniques – Write down your goals and ensure they are fulfilling the SMART technique:
- S – Specific
- M – Measurable
- A – Achievable
- R -Realistic
- T – Timebound

Affirmations – Write down three affirmations that are most suited for your purpose in life:

1)
_____
_____
_____

2)
_____
_____
_____

3)
_____
_____
_____

Visualization – Rate the following goals in order of the

importance in your life:

- Graduating from college
- Getting a medal in an important sports event
- Being financially successful in life
- Traveling the world
- Becoming a successful musician

Now, for the first two goals visualize a successful end result and write them down in detail. If none of the above-mentioned goals are in your list, then go ahead and make your own choices.

Workbook for the Practice of Personal Integrity

NLP Techniques – Look at the following examples of how to say no politely, and rank them in the order of your preference from the most liked to the least liked. Then practice using them, and don't forget to say no when you are sure you cannot keep promises:

- This is not a good fit for me
- Sounds interesting, but right now I'm really pressed for time
- I am afraid I'll have to pass up your invitation this time
- If I agreed to help you, I will be forced to break my promise
- Sorry, this doesn't fit my schedule

Affirmations – Write down three affirmations that are most suitable for your lifestyle:

1)

_____

_____

_____

2)

_____

_____

_____

3)

_____

_____

_____

Maintaining a Diary – Think of two of the most embarrassing times in your life when you did not keep your promises. Now, answer the following questions based on those experiences:

What were reasons for you to break the promise?

_____

_____

_____

_____

_____

What were your feelings?

_____

_____

_____

_____

_____

What lessons have you learned from those experiences which helped you grow your personal integrity?

_____

_____

_____

Chapter 6: Conclusion

The most crucial lesson in your journey of building and developing self-esteem is the fact that it is a never-ending journey. You can never reach a situation where you can say that you have nothing more to do in terms of building your self-esteem. Each stage in your life will bring new challenges which could affect your self-esteem, and you might need to start again from scratch.

You have to continuously upgrade your knowledge and skills regarding the basic components of self-esteem that are discussed in this book including:

- Living consciously
- Self-acceptance
- Self-responsibility
- Self-assertiveness
- Living with purpose
- Personal integrity

As you grow from a teenager into an adult and face the challenges of the wide world outside, you will be grateful for having become aware of the importance of self-esteem and its components early on in life. Not many people are fortunate enough to have got the insight to develop this crucial personality trait from the age of adolescence.

The habits learned and mastered during your adolescence will get so deeply embedded in your psyche that they will always be part of your system. So, picking up good habits during your teenage days is the best way to keep them in your long-term memory.

Confidence, self-esteem, and assertiveness are all related and yet different from each other. The main focus of this part was on Self Esteem.

So, go ahead and start your journey of self-discovery to build and develop your self-esteem. Be prepared to keep learning and moving forward.

25375583R00132

Made in the USA
San Bernardino, CA
11 February 2019